40 HIKES in

TENNESSEE'S
SOUTH CUMBERLAND

40 HIKES in

TENNESSEE'S
SOUTH CUMBERLAND

THIRD EDITION
Russ Manning

THE
MOUNTAINEERS

For Gary and Jason

Published by
The Mountaineers
1001 SW Klickitat Way, Suite 201
Seattle, WA 98134

Third edition, 2000. First edition, 1990 as *The South Cumberland and Fall Creek Falls*. Second edition, 1994 as *Tennessee's South Cumberland* by Russ Manning and Sondra Jamieson.

Published simultaneously in Great Britain by Cordee, 3a DeMontfort Street, Leicester, England, LE1 7HD

Manufactured in the United States of America

Project Editor: Christine Ummel Hosler
Editor: Carol Peschke
Maps by Mark Stout, Jerry Painter
All photographs by Russ Manning unless otherwise noted
Cover and book design by Jennifer LaRock Shontz
Book layout by Amy Winchester

Cover photograph: *Buzzard Point at the Laurel–Snow Pocket Wilderness*
Frontispiece: *Suter Falls*

Library of Congress Cataloging-in-Publication Data
Manning, Russ.
    40 hikes in Tennessee's South Cumberland / by Russ Manning.—3rd ed.
        p.   cm.
    Rev. ed. of: The South Cumberland and Fall Creek Falls recreation area and state park / by Russ Manning and Sondra Jamieson. ©1990.
    Includes index.
    ISBN 0-89886-637-5 (pbk.)
    1. Hiking—Tennessee—South Cumberland Recreation Area—Guidebooks.
2. Hiking—Tennessee—Fall Creek Falls State Park—Guidebooks. 3. Trails—Tennessee—South Cumberland Recreation Area—Guidebooks. 4. Trails—Tennessee—Fall Creek Falls State Park—Guidebooks. 5. South Cumberland Recreation Area (Tenn.)—Guidebooks. 6. Fall Creek Falls State Park (Tenn.)—Guidebooks. I. Title: Forty hikes in Tennessee's South Cumberland. II. Manning, Russ. South Cumberland and Fall Creek Falls recreation area and state park. III. Title.
GV199.42.T22 S664 1999
917.68'70453—dc21   99-050630
                                                                            CIP

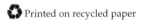

CONTENTS

State Parks and Natural Areas of the South Cumberland

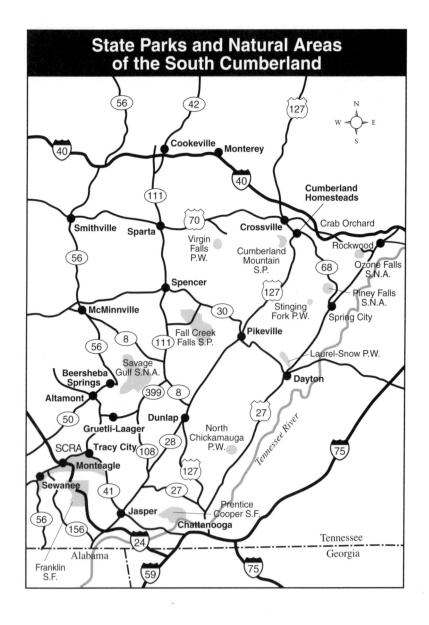

CUMBERLAND MOUNTAIN STATE RUSTIC PARK AND SURROUNDING AREA (MAP 4)

WALDEN RIDGE NORTH (MAP 5)

LAUREL–SNOW POCKET WILDERNESS (MAP 6)

NORTH CHICKAMAUGA POCKET WILDERNESS (MAP 7)

PRENTICE COOPER STATE FOREST AND WILDLIFE MANAGEMENT AREA (MAP 8)

Key to Map Symbols and Abbreviations

——	Interstate highway, US and state highways	⊼	Picnic area
══	Unpaved road	⇧	Visitor center
-------	Trail	(75)	Interstate highway
∿	River/stream	(340)	US highway
⌐	Plateau/gulf/gorge rim	(622)	State highway
— – —	Park boundary	S.P.	State Park
40	Hike number	P.W.	Pocket Wilderness
▲	Campground	S.F.	State Forest
♦	Entrance station	S.N.A.	State Natural Area
■	Building	SCRA	South Cumberland Recreation Area

ACKNOWLEDGMENTS

I am grateful to the staff of the South Cumberland Recreation Area (SCRA) for their support in the preparation of this book. Park manager John Christof encouraged the effort and former ranger–naturalist Randy Hedgepath provided invaluable aid in my exploration of the lands that make up the SCRA, guiding me on several walks, giving advice, and answering questions. Former ranger Wayne Morrison took the time to guide me to Suter Falls and answer questions. I was impressed with the dedication and diverse contributions of these and the rest of the SCRA staff.

I thank those who reviewed all or part of draft manuscripts: Randy Hedgepath at the SCRA; superintendent A. J. Anderson and interpretive specialist Stuart Carroll of Fall Creek Falls State Park; superintendent Andy Lyon of Cumberland Mountain State Rustic Park; Craig Earnest, land management coordinator in the Alabama/Georgia region; Tom Mainor, senior forest supervisor of the Southeastern Tennessee Region; David Smith, timberlands manager for the Bowater Incorporated Calhoun Woodlands Operations; and Herman Baggenstoss, who was the guiding power behind the creation of the SCRA. Park manager John Christof provided information for this third edition.

I also thank Bob Brown of the Tennessee Trails Association for information on the Cumberland Trail.

PREFACE

Every place has its special attraction. The forested mountains that make up the Great Smoky Mountains National Park in east Tennessee and North Carolina display vibrant color in the fall and a multitude of wildflowers in the spring. The Big South Fork National River and Recreation Area on the northern part of the Cumberland Plateau in Tennessee and Kentucky includes a river gorge with sheer rock walls in places.

For the South Cumberland, the southern part of Tennessee's Cumberland Plateau that is also dissected with deep gorges, it's the waterfalls. There's Suter, Virgin, Greeter, Savage, Stinging Fork, Cane Creek, Fall Creek, Piney, Upper Piney, Lower Piney, Rockhouse, Ozone, Snow, Sycamore, Foster, Tom Pack, Horsepound, Bridal Veil, Pine Branch, Big Laurel, Laurel, and Laurel again. The state of Tennessee has set aside many of these waterfalls

Stone Door Overlook

and gorges of the South Cumberland in a state recreation area, state parks and forests, and state natural areas—places where you can hike and camp or just picnic and take a short walk to an overlook.

Years ago, when I first began exploring the trails into the South Cumberland, I not only learned to cherish this land but also became intrigued with the history of the area. It has since become one of my favorite places because of this combination of history and the outdoors, and because of the separateness. Although the South Cumberland is only a 2- or 3-hour drive from several urban areas, it remains a place apart. Here you'll experience a sense of isolation in the deep gorges set among historic towns and farmlands. Perhaps *insulation* is a better word: You'll find yourself insulated from the harried activities that fill most people's lives.

On the South Cumberland you can slow down, take your time, travel into the past or into the wilderness. In this guide, I give you a little history and tell you about the trails where you can see the wilderness for yourself.

INTRODUCTION

The Cumberland Plateau country was first inhabited by prehistoric Native American peoples who lived in the numerous rock shelters and gathered food from the forests and the rivers. By the beginning of recorded history, the Cherokees dominated the region in Tennessee. Coming from their towns in the river valleys to the southeast, they hunted the plateau, camping along the streams and under rock shelters.

Apart from the long hunters who occasionally penetrated the plateau region, the first white people to encounter the plateau were immigrants traveling west to settle the Cumberland River Valley in middle Tennessee. Eventually settlements sprang up along the roads and trails that crossed the plateau. Pressure from these early settlers and others who wanted

All Saints' Chapel at Sewanee

Cherokee lands led to several treaties in the late 1700s and early 1800s in which the Cherokees were persuaded to give up their claim to the region. In the intervening years, villages and towns arose on the Cumberland Plateau. Many people were attracted by the untouched timber and the coal that underlies much of the region. Others came to start small farms.

Because the Cumberland Plateau was a pristine land, it offered the promise of new beginnings. Several historic communities formed out of the dreams of the people who came.

The town of Tracy City grew up around the mining and railroad operations of the Sewanee Mining Company that began in the 1850s. The company built a spur off the Nashville and Chattanooga Railroad from Cowan up the mountain to the city, which was named for the president of the new company, Samuel F. Tracy. The company grew into the Tennessee Coal, Iron, and Railroad Company. Until about 1900, coal mining was a profitable enterprise in and around the community.

In the late 1800s, John Moffat founded the community of Monteagle. Moffat was concerned about the lack of education in the region and helped establish the Fairmount Female College in Monteagle, which eventually became the DuBose Episcopal Conference Center. Moffat also donated land to form the Moffat Collegiate and Normal Institute for the training of teachers. Never successful, the school became the Monteagle Sunday School Assembly for the training of Sunday school teachers. Today, the assembly is a 90-acre enclave of elaborate summer homes and cottages that still has a season of programs and lectures. Visitors can stay at North Gate Lodge or Edgeworth Inn.

Leonidas Polk, Episcopal bishop of Arkansas and Louisiana, first had the vision of a University of the South, which was founded 1857–58 on 10,000 acres of land at Sewanee, the Indian name for the area. The land on which the Episcopal university stands, part of which was donated by the Sewanee Mining Company, is called the Domain and still comprises one of the largest university campuses in the world.

Beginning in 1844, Switzerland experienced a great depression, and many Swiss immigrated to the United States; several were encouraged to settle on the Cumberland Plateau. The community they formed was called Gruetli, after a high mountain meadow in Switzerland where the Swiss declared their independence from Austria in 1291. About 100 families originally settled the community, which eventually merged with another community to become Gruetli–Laager.

Louise and John Baggenstoss came to Tennessee to settle near the Gruetli Swiss colony and founded the Baggenstoss Bakery in Tracy City in 1902. Their six sons, John, Robert, Herman, Fritz, Charlie, and Albert, eventually operated the bakery, changing the name to Dutch Maid Bakery. Lynn Craig took over the management with the death of Albert, who had been the official Dutch Maid Baker. With some of the Baggenstoss family still actively involved, it is the oldest family bakery in Tennessee and is known for its sweet rolls, cookies, sugar plum cake, and fresh-from-the-oven sourdough and salt-rising bread.

In 1833 Beersheba Porter Cain and her husband, John, established a resort community at the edge of the plateau around a spring of iron water she thought had medicinal value. Beersheba Springs expanded under several owners. After the Civil War, the resort did not regain its popularity. The hotel and guest cottages built in the early years became a United Methodist Church Assembly. The community still contains many elegant summer homes and cottages.

During the Great Depression of the 1930s, the Subsistence Homesteads Project financed the building of a homestead settlement on the upper end of the South Cumberland. The Cumberland Homesteads consisted of new houses built on subsistence farms. The town is distinctive because most of the buildings and original homes were constructed of the local Crab Orchard sandstone.

STATE PARKS AND FORESTS ARE FORMED

The South Cumberland is arbitrarily the part of the Cumberland Plateau in Tennessee that extends from Crossville south toward Chattanooga. For most of its length, Tennessee's South Cumberland is bisected by the 70-mile-long Sequatchie Valley. The finger of plateau that remains on the east is commonly called Walden Ridge, after one of the early explorers, and the west side is considered the Cumberland Plateau proper.

Set on this divided tableland are several state parks, forests, and natural areas. One of the largest preserves is the South Cumberland Recreation Area (SCRA).

The places that make up the SCRA had for many years been favorite haunts of local people who enjoyed the outdoors and a few people from outside the area who had heard about the hiking opportunities. Wanting to permanently protect some of these areas, local conservationists, including the Grundy County Conservation Board headed by Herman Baggenstoss, approached the state of Tennessee about forming several state parks. The response was that most were too small. The solution worked out between the conservationists and the state—with the organizational and planning support of the Tennessee Valley Authority (TVA), the federal agency that is the primary utility in Tennessee—was to combine the several areas into one park system.

Established in 1978, the SCRA now consists of eight areas totaling 13,064 acres scattered over a 100-square-mile region. The primary unit is Savage Gulf State Natural Area, with its 11,500 acres. The smaller parcels include the 140-acre Mr. & Mrs. Harry Lee Carter State Natural Area, which contains the Buggytop Trail to Lost Cove Cave; the 150-acre Grundy Lakes State Park, site of the Lone Rock Coke Ovens; the 212-acre Grundy Forest State Natural Area and 178-acre Foster Falls TVA Small Wild Area, with a 500-acre addition, which are connected by the near-famous Fiery Gizzard

North Gate Lodge in Monteagle

Trail; the 1.5-acre Sewanee Natural Bridge State Natural Area, with its 27-foot-high sandstone arch; and the 250-acre Hawkins Cove State Natural Area, which preserves the rare Cumberland rosinweed. The SCRA is served by a visitor center located on US 41 between Tracy City and Monteagle in the 136-acre South Cumberland State Park.

Because of its size and its ecological importance, the Savage Gulf area has had its own preservation effort. The Savage Gulf Preservation League has worked many years for the protection of the area. Savage Gulf State Natural Area consists of three 5-mile gorges, called gulfs by Tennesseans. Savage Creek and Big Creek flow down two side gulfs to merge with the Collins River, which has carved the middle gulf. The three gulfs reach depths of 800 feet.

The Preservation League mounted an effort to protect the scenic beauty of the area and to preserve an unlogged stretch of land in the depths of Savage Gulf, 500 acres of old-growth timber that is one of the largest remaining stands of mixed mesophytic forest in the eastern United States and is now designated a National Natural Landmark. The state of Tennessee acquired Savage Gulf in 1973; the Stone Door area had been acquired in 1969. The Nature Conservancy stepped in to help by acquiring some of the land in Big Creek and Collins Gulfs from the Huber Lumber Company, which made a significant donation by selling at less than appraised value. The Nature Conservancy preserved the land until the state could purchase it with a matching federal grant. The state subsequently acquired other areas to complete Savage Gulf State Natural Area, the premier wilderness area on the Cumberland Plateau.

Just north of Savage Gulf and the SCRA lies the 21,000-acre Fall Creek Falls State Park and Natural Area. The state park has an inn, cabins, golf course, tennis courts, and shopping village. But the park also contains Cane Creek Gorge, which offers the same type of scenic and wilderness attractions as the SCRA.

The park was established in 1935 when the federal government created the Fall Creek Falls National Recreation Demonstration Area. Much of the acreage had been logged, burned over, and converted to pasture. The plan was to make it into a wildlife sanctuary. In 1944 the Department of the Interior deeded the park to the state of Tennessee and it became Fall Creek Falls State Park. Land was added, roads improved, and facilities constructed to make it accessible. In 1972, additional improvements and facilities, equally funded by the state and the Economic Development Administration, brought the park up to the status of a state resort park.

To the credit of the park planners, all the accommodations and recreational facilities are confined to the plateau area. Cane Creek Gorge and its tributary gorges remain virtual wilderness with pockets of unlogged forest and small isolated coves. Several waterfalls head these gorges, including 256-foot-high Fall Creek Falls, the tallest waterfall in the eastern United States.

Other areas, smaller preserves, are scattered across the South Cumberland. There's Cumberland Mountain State Rustic Park to the north of Fall Creek Falls State Park. This 1,720-acre park was originally a recreation area for the surrounding Cumberland Homesteads, a community created during the New Deal era. Facilities in the park were built by the Civilian Conservation Corps and the Work Projects Administration and opened to the public in 1940. Most of the buildings were constructed of the local Crab Orchard sandstone.

There are also state forests. Tennessee created Franklin State Forest out of 6,941 acres purchased from the Cross Creek Coal Company in 1936. Prentice Cooper State Forest, named for a former state governor, contains 26,000 acres (acquired in several pieces) and was established in 1945. Ozone Falls and Piney Falls State Natural Areas were also established by the state to protect scenic areas.

In addition to state-run areas, private lands belonging to Bowater

Incorporated, a paper company, are open to the public. Bowater Calhoun Woodlands Operations manages about 340,000 acres of timberlands in Tennessee. In 1967 Bowater began encouraging the public to visit certain of its lands set aside as areas of scenic and geological significance. The corporation constructed hiking trails into these areas, to which it gave the designation *pocket wilderness*. Four of these small wilderness areas are located on the South Cumberland: Virgin Falls, Stinging Fork, Laurel–Snow, and North Chickamauga. In addition to the Bowater wilderness designation, these areas are registered state natural areas.

GETTING THERE

Tennessee's South Cumberland lies between Knoxville and Nashville south of I-40. Traveling from the east on the interstate, you'll encounter the Cumberland Plateau at the Harriman–Rockwood exit and make a long climb along I-40 to the top. From the west, you'll reach the foot of the plateau and ascend toward Monterey, which sits on the western edge. At this latitude, the plateau stretches about 45 miles from rim to rim.

From the south or the west, you can approach the South Cumberland along I-24, which connects Chattanooga and Nashville. Northwest of Chattanooga, the interstate passes through Monteagle, with the SCRA Visitor Center 3.6 miles to the east on US 41; watch for a turn northeast in Monteagle to stay with US 41.

The main artery through the South Cumberland is the highway that runs nearly the length of Sequatchie Valley. US 127 extends south from I-40 through Crossville, past the Cumberland Homesteads and Cumberland Mountain State Park, and then drops into Sequatchie Valley. At Pikeville, you can turn northwest on TN 30 to get to the north entrance of Fall Creek Falls State Park. The north entrance can also be reached from the town of Spencer on the west; you can take TN 111 south from I-40 at Cookeville and then turn east on TN 30 in Spencer.

South of Pikeville on US 127, just north of Dunlap, you can turn northwest on TN 8/111 to a left turn on TN 399 to get to the Savage Gulf Entrance to the Savage Gulf State Natural Area. The Stone Door Entrance to Savage Gulf is best approached from the McMinnville side of the natural area along TN 56 at Beersheba Springs. On TN 8/111 you can also continue north past where TN 8 turns off and continue on TN 111 to enter Fall Creek Falls State Park at its south entrance.

At Dunlap, US 127 veers southeast toward Chattanooga, so you'll have to bear right on TN 28 to continue down Sequatchie Valley. At Jasper, you can turn north on US 41 to Tracy City and the SCRA Visitor Center 3.2 miles beyond.

GEOLOGY

At one time, ocean covered a portion of what is now Tennessee. Great deltas formed where rivers flowing from Appalachian highlands to the east

Getting to the South Cumberland

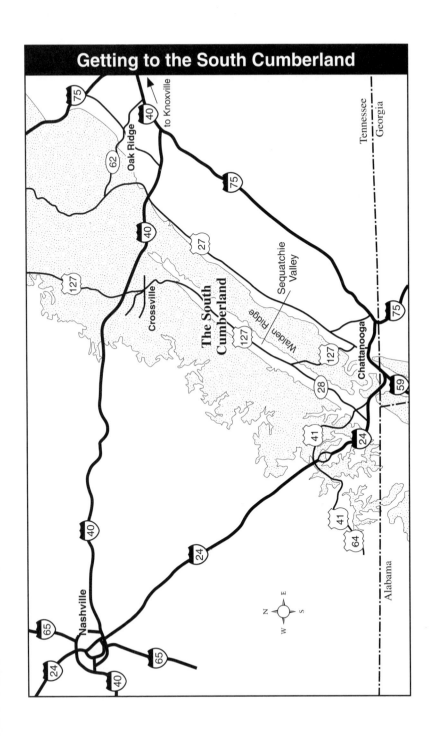

met this inland sea along a shoreline in the area that would become the Cumberland Plateau.

About 300 million years ago, a final episode of Appalachian mountain building resulted from the collision of the African and North American continental plates. The new mountains that formed in the east eroded quickly, depositing a layer of sand and gravel more than a hundred feet thick over the entire delta system of what was to be the plateau region. Later, the shoreline settled and the sea reinvaded, dropping its silt. This cycle of mountain building to the east, followed by erosion and deposition of sediment, repeated in several pulses over millions of years during a time geologists call the Pennsylvanian Period.

Under the increasing weight, these piled-up layers consolidated into rock, becoming layers of shale, siltstone, clay, and sandstone. The thick sand and gravel layer first laid down became a very erosion-resistant Pennsylvanian sandstone.

Then later, as erosion swept away overlying layers, the land rose high above sea level in three intervals of secondary uplift. The repeated uplift thrusts occurred as less dense rock below was forced upward by surrounding dense rock. Erosion immediately began lowering these new mountains in the plateau region. But the erosion slowed when it encountered the resistant Pennsylvanian sandstone, so after millions of years of erosion a plateau still stands 2,000 feet above sea level. This plateau, which stretches from Kentucky through Tennessee and into Alabama, was named the Cumberland Plateau by early explorers.

The plateau was once overlain by eroded beds of soil and silt. To the north, these partially remain as the Cumberland Mountains. To the south, this sedimentary material has eroded away, leaving the hard Pennsylvanian sandstone as the surface rock of a tableland of broad plains dissected by river gorges.

As the force of the continental collision moved from southeast to northwest, it bent the Pennsylvanian sandstone, producing such tension that the rock sometimes broke. Parts of the plateau were shoved northwest, and older rock deep in the earth to the southeast was laid over younger rock nearer the surface to the northwest. Geologists call this the Cumberland Plateau overthrust fault.

To the southwest in Tennessee, the overthrust system formed a great arch, part of which remains as the Crab Orchard Mountains. Southwest of these mountains the rock was so broken that erosion was able to wear away the ridge and then dip out a long, straight depression following the line of the arch, creating Sequatchie Valley, which divides the South Cumberland, with Walden Ridge to the east and the bulk of the plateau to the west.

In much of the remainder of the South Cumberland, the Pennsylvanian caprock is still intact, in places reaching a thickness of hundreds of feet. Where erosion has taken advantage of a crack in this capstone, a dramatic landscape has resulted, making the South Cumberland a land of geological wonder.

Streams and rivers cut deep, steep-walled gorges as they run their courses. From the sandstone rim of a gorge, it's usually a 100- to 200-foot drop to a forest and rubble zone that slopes steeply to the edge of the stream in the center of the gorge.

Where streams flow over breaks in the sandstone, they quickly carry away the broken pieces of caprock and scoop out softer layers below, forming the numerous waterfalls to be found on the South Cumberland. The sandstone lip that forms the top of a waterfall resists breaking off, so the erosion of plunging water, mist, and spray has time to gouge at the softer rock layers under and behind the waterfall until a deep plunge pool is formed with an amphitheater behind, which is why it is possible to walk behind most waterfalls on the plateau.

The best way to explore this land is by walking. Hiking trails lead to overlooks that present magnificent views of some of the deepest gorges in the eastern United States. Trails wander by waterfalls that sail off sandstone ledges to drop into cool, green pools or disappear into subterranean passages where erosion has reached limestone layers. These trails and the sights they include make the South Cumberland a special place for hiking in the Southeast.

FLORA AND FAUNA

An uplands forest grows on the surface of the Cumberland Plateau. Primarily pine and oak stand in the shallow, sandy soils where white-tailed deer follow ancient game trails. Hairy woodpeckers, common flickers, and pileated woodpeckers search the trees for insects while the pine warbler, evening grosbeak, and white-breasted nuthatch forage for conifer seeds. Crows and a variety of hawks skim the tree tops. Gray squirrels scurry up the trunks of trees while below bobwhite, turkey, eastern chipmunk, white-footed mouse, and eastern cottontail hide among the bushes.

The gorges of the South Cumberland are occupied by a more varied forest, a complex association called the Ravine Forest in which several tree species dominate.

The canopy layer of the Ravine Forest includes beech, sugar maple, red oak, tulip poplar, white oak, hemlock, birch, black cherry, white ash, red maple, cucumber magnolia, sycamore, and hickory. The understory is dogwood, hophornbeam, sourwood, holly, redbud, ironwood, serviceberry, sassafras. The shrubs are rhododendron, mountain laurel, wild azalea. The forest floor is covered with a variety of ferns and, in season, wildflowers that include asters, common cinquefoil, trailing arbutus, goldenrods, violets, showy orchis, trillium, phacelia, phlox, wild iris, toothwort, spring beauty, bloodroot, and fire pink.

Not all species occur in any single area. Distinct communities have developed in which only some species are present because of variations in soil, moisture, elevation, and slope exposure. But the overall climax forest consists of these individual communities.

From the rim, the nearly bare walls of the gorges drop straight down to the forest below. In a few cracks and crevices grow alum root, ferns, and scraggly pines. Vultures, phoebes, and swallows occasionally find nesting places, and a solitary bat can be found beneath an overhang or in a cave beneath the sandstone layer. From a perch on the rim, the red-tailed, broad-winged, and sharp-shinned hawks gaze into the depths of the gorge. The timber rattler and northern copperhead lie on the warm bare rocks in the afternoon sun.

Below the gorge walls, mixed oak communities cover south-facing slopes. Here the dense undergrowth and abundant mast attract the ruffed grouse, turkey, opossum, and gray squirrel. The smaller animals include the short-tailed shrew, eastern chipmunk, deer mouse, and eastern mole. The wood thrush, downy woodpecker, and hooded warbler inhabit the understory, and the red-eyed vireo, scarlet tanager, and tufted titmouse live in the canopy.

The north-facing slopes have shaded coves of hemlock, rhododendron, and partridgeberry, virtually isolated except for a passing deer, bobcat, or red fox and the blackpoll warbler and golden-crowned kinglet feeding in the canopy.

The low, moist slopes are covered in the classic mixed mesophytic forest, where several hardwood species dominate: sugar maple, beech, tulip poplar, basswood, ash, and buckeye. The forest is inhabited by the gray fox, striped skunk, eastern wood rat, and grouse, turkey, and squirrel. The birds here include warblers, hawks, owls, and vireos.

Along the floor of the gorge, an alluvial forest of sycamore and river birch, with ash and alder, shelters muskrat, raccoon, and rarely, mink and otter. Along the shore can be found Louisiana waterthrush, American woodcock, wood ducks, and herons.

In the floodplain and associated ponds and puddles, reptiles and amphibians live with the fluctuating river: southern leopard frogs, red-spotted newts, northern water snakes, spotted salamanders, and eastern box turtles. In the river and tributary creeks, largemouth and smallmouth bass, bluegill, darters, creek chub, and shiner minnows are supported by an association of diatoms, algae, zooplankton, and aquatic insects.

All of these communities of plants and animals, from the gorge rim to the water's edge, intrude and overlap, mingling to create the Ravine Forest of the South Cumberland.

HIKING THE SOUTH CUMBERLAND

The best times to hike the South Cumberland are the spring and fall, when the temperatures are mild and the forest is dressed in a variety of wildflowers or autumn color. You might start your exploration at the SCRA Visitor

Center on US 41, where you can gather information and walk the 2-mile Meadow Trails complex that offers pleasant strolls through meadows and woodlands characteristic of the plateau tableland.

Most trails on the South Cumberland are blazed white, but some state parks, such as Fall Creek Falls and Cumberland Mountain, use blazes of various colors.

Preparations

Even if you are out for only a short walk, you should wear walking shoes or hiking boots, which are designed to give sure footing and to support ankles. For day hikes, carry a pack with water, a lunch or snacks, and rain gear; it rains frequently on the South Cumberland in the winter and spring. In summer, throw in some insect repellent and sunscreen. Take along a plastic sheet or emergency blanket in case of emergency. Always bring the Ten Essentials: a topographic map and compass, extra clothes, extra food, sunglasses, a knife, a flashlight with fresh batteries, a lighter or matches in a waterproof container, firestarter, and a first-aid kit. If you are backpacking, you need everything for surviving in the open overnight; if you are inexperienced, the rangers at one of the parks or your local outfitting store can give advice on the equipment needed.

Once at the trailhead, you should be able to find your way using the book's descriptions and the signs at most trail junctions. But you must assume responsibility for knowing where you are going and for not getting lost. Always let someone know where you are going and give an expected return time so he or she can contact park authorities if you don't return. To keep from getting lost, read trail signs, stay on the trails, and don't overestimate your ability. If you get lost, do not leave the trail; search teams will cover the trails first when looking for you.

The maps in this book are designed to help in finding the trailheads and showing the general route and trail connections; they are not designed for detailed navigating. For more detailed information, check the topographical maps that cover the area you will be hiking, available from your local map supplier. Trail maps of the various state parks and forests are available at their visitor centers or headquarters. Maps of the pocket wilderness trails are available from Bowater Calhoun Woodlands Operations; of the Grassy Cove section of the Cumberland Trail, from Cumberland Mountain State Park; and of the Perimeter Trail, from the Sewanee Outing Program at the University of the South.

Precautions

Take care of the land. Do not pick wildflowers. Leave historic and archaeological sites, including rock shelters and other natural features, undisturbed.

And take care of yourself; be especially careful climbing on rocks, hiking along the edge of bluffs, and crossing streams. Do not climb on waterfalls.

You are expected to take responsibility for your own safety, keeping in mind that hiking in a wilderness setting far from medical attention is an inherently hazardous activity. Hike with someone; that way if one of you is injured, someone will be there to care for the injured person and to go for help.

All water in the backcountry should be considered contaminated. Boil water for at least 2 minutes before drinking it to destroy bacteria and other microorganisms, including *Giardia lamblia,* a flagellate protozoan that causes an intestinal disorder called giardiasis.

Rarely, you may encounter a timber rattler or a northern copperhead. Watch where you put your feet and hands, and if you must walk through brush, explore ahead with a stick. If you do encounter snakes, leave them alone; they belong there.

Watch for ticks; one type, the deer tick, can transmit a spirochete that causes Lyme disease. Although Lyme disease is uncommon in the Southeast, you should remain vigilant in keeping ticks off yourself and checking for ticks after a hike.

You may encounter poison ivy along an overgrown trail. Watch for the three-leaf clusters and avoid contact if possible. Long pants will prevent contact.

After a heavy rain, streams can be swollen with rushing water. Do not

A ranger-led hike

attempt to ford such a stream unless you are sure you can make it. When the water level is down, you can rockhop most creeks, but this can also be hazardous if the rocks are wet and slippery; use caution. If you decide to wade across, wear your shoes to protect your feet; some hikers carry along old tennis shoes or sandals for stream crossings. Find a branch to use for balance if you do not have a walking stick. Carrying a backpack, release the hip belt so you can easily slip out of the pack if you fall in the water. If you do take a dunking and the water carries you away, orient to float on your back with your feet downstream so you can ward off rocks until you have a chance to stop yourself and get out of the water. Even when you are crossing a footbridge over a creek you should use caution; some can be wet and slippery or covered with ice in winter.

In cold and wet weather, you face the danger of hypothermia, the lowering of core temperature beyond the point at which the body can maintain its own heat. The symptoms are uncontrolled shivering, slurred speech, memory lapse, stumbling, fumbling hands, and drowsiness. Hypothermia can occur in any season and can result in death. If you are wet and cold, get under some shelter and change into dry clothes. If you begin to experience symptoms, get into a sleeping bag, if available. Drink warm fluids to raise the core temperature of your body. Some hikers, feeling the symptoms of hypothermia, begin running to increase their body heat, but you should attempt this only in the early stages when you are coherent. To prevent hypothermia, stay dry, eat even if you are not hungry so your body will have fuel from which to produce heat, and drink water even when you are not thirsty so your body can assimilate your food.

Hunting is allowed in and around parts of the SCRA, in Franklin and Prentice Cooper State Forests, in the portion of Fall Creek Falls that is a wildlife management area, and near Bowater pocket wilderness areas. The state forests can provide a hunting season schedule. You can also check with the various visitor centers to find out whether hunting is going on when you want to hike, and whether you should avoid certain areas or wear orange clothing. Pets are allowed on trails in the South Cumberland but should always be kept on a leash; consider leaving them at home.

Camping

There are campgrounds at Fall Creek Falls and Cumberland Mountain State Parks and at Foster Falls TVA Small Wild Area.

Backcountry camping is by permit only and in designated areas in the SCRA and at Fall Creek Falls and Cumberland Mountain State Parks. Register at the park visitor centers and, for Savage Gulf State Natural Area, at the ranger stations at the Savage Gulf and Stone Door Entrances. Permits are not required for camping at Bowater pocket wilderness areas and at the state forests; you may camp anywhere at Franklin but only in designated places at Prentice Cooper and the pocket wildernesses. Select campsites for minimal impact.

When campsites are not designated, plan to camp near a large stream to be guaranteed of a source of water; streams are noted in the descriptions and the maps. You can also carry water from these streams while you are hiking during the day. Any streams noted in this book that you step across, and even some larger, will almost surely be dry during the less rainy seasons, so plan ahead and carry water with you. Hang food out of reach of animals, at least 4 feet from the tree trunk and 10 feet from the ground.

When backcountry toilets are not available, bury your waste at least 6 inches deep and away from trails and campsites; be sure you are at least 200 feet from all water sources. Do not bury toilet paper, sanitary napkins, or tampons; instead, add them to your trash bag and carry them out. Check whether campfires are safe and permitted in the area you intend to hike; if so, use only down and dead timber. Keep fires small and build only in existing fire rings. Consider using a stove even where wood fires are permitted. Do not wash dishes in a stream; take water from the streams to do your washing and let the waste water drain onto the ground. Use the same procedure if you plan to bathe with soap instead of just splashing around in the water. Pack out all trash.

HOW TO USE THIS BOOK

For each trail description in this book, the distance is given. The hikes range from short walks to long backpacking trails. For those who prefer short hikes, the distance is sometimes given to an attraction part way that can be your destination.

The trails are rated easy, moderate, or strenuous. This degree of difficulty is based on the ability of an average person, so experienced hikers may find the moderate trails fairly easy and the strenuous trails only moderate. The rating is primarily a subjective judgment of the difficulty of the trail—how much up and down there is, how difficult the stream crossings are, and whether the footing on the trail is rocky.

The elevation gain or loss listed indicates a difference in elevation between the trail's highest and lowest points. I use *elevation change* on a loop trail because you will gain and lose the same elevation along a loop hike. I also use *elevation change* when the hike is one way but the trail descends into a gorge and then comes back to the plateau rim, or does the reverse; in either case, you both ascend and descend while hiking the trail just one way. Be aware that there could be several ups and downs along the way in addition to the listed elevation change, so you can ascend and descend a total of many more feet than indicated.

Cautions, or warnings, are listed about what you might encounter on the trail, such as creek crossings, rocky footing, mudholes, and steep climbs and descents. When deciding whether you're up to hiking a particular trail, take these cautions into consideration and be prepared.

For those who want to hike farther, trail connections are included so you can combine several trails for longer walks. Many of these combinations are quite long, so you need to be in good shape for walking the total mileage in a single day or plan to camp in the backcountry.

In the narrative description, the mileages are almost always cumulative. If you want to hike the trail in the reverse direction from the description, it might be helpful to calculate the reverse mileages so you can more easily keep track of how far you have walked and how far you have to go.

The maps accompanying the trail descriptions in this book are labeled with the corresponding trail numbers.

A NOTE ABOUT SAFETY

Safety is an important concern in all outdoor activities. No guidebook can alert you to every hazard or anticipate the limitations of every reader. Therefore, the descriptions of roads, trails, routes, and natural features in this book are not representations that a particular place or excursion will be safe for your party. When you follow any of the routes described in this book, you assume responsibility for your own safety. Under normal conditions, such excursions require the usual attention to traffic, road and trail conditions, weather, terrain, the capabilities of your party, and other factors. Because many of the lands in this book are subject to development and/or change of ownership, conditions may have changed since this book was written that make your use of some of these routes unwise. Always check for current conditions, obey posted private property signs, and avoid confrontations with property owners or managers. Keeping informed on current conditions and exercising common sense are the keys to a safe, enjoyable outing.

—*The Mountaineers*

Map 1. South Cumberland Recreation Area and Nearby Trails

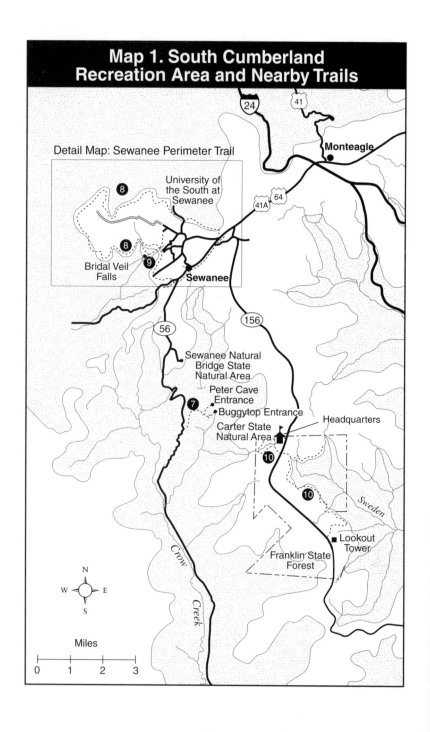

Detail Map: Sewanee Perimeter Trail

University of the South at Sewanee

Monteagle

Bridal Veil Falls

Sewanee

Sewanee Natural Bridge State Natural Area

Peter Cave Entrance

Buggytop Entrance

Carter State Natural Area

Headquarters

Franklin State Forest

Lookout Tower

Sweden

Crow Creek

N
W E
S

Miles
0   1   2   3

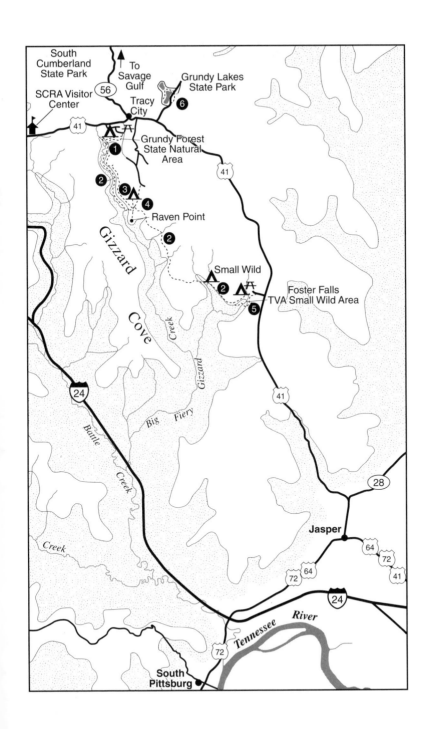

SOUTH CUMBERLAND RECREATION AREA AND NEARBY TRAILS

Though not well known outside the region, Tennessee's South Cumberland Recreation Area (SCRA) is one of the most interesting areas in the Southeast for hiking. Trails lead to Lost Cove Cave, historic coke ovens, a natural arch, and numerous waterfalls and gorge overlooks. The challenging Fiery Gizzard Trail, linking the Grundy Forest State Natural Area and the Foster Falls TVA Small Wild Area, is gradually developing a reputation as one of the best trails in the region. Outside the recreation area, other trails loop around the historic domain of the nearby University of the South and penetrate Franklin State Forest.

Between Chattanooga and Nashville, I-24 climbs the Cumberland Plateau to pass over a narrow arm of the plateau at Monteagle. From here the Sewanee Natural Bridge State Natural Area, Carter State Natural Area, Franklin State Forest, and the University of the South lie to the southeast on US 64/41A. To the east on US 41 lie South Cumberland State Park, Grundy Forest State Natural Area, Grundy Lakes State Park, and Foster Falls TVA Small Wild Area. Begin your exploration of the region at the SCRA Visitor Center, located at South Cumberland State Park 3.6 miles to the east on US 41.

1 GRUNDY FOREST DAY LOOP

Distance: 2.0-mile loop
Difficulty: Moderate
Elevation Change: 100 ft
Cautions: Stream crossing, rough footing, steep banks
Connections: Fiery Gizzard Trail

Attractions: This trail into the head of Gizzard Cove meanders through giant hemlocks and offers views of waterfalls, cascades, and the junction of the Big and Little Fiery Gizzard Creeks. In spring, the area flaunts displays of hepatica, phacelia, geranium, crested dwarf iris, trillium, and wild phlox. Camping is available at the Civilian Conservation Corps (CCC) Campsite.

How the creeks got the name *Fiery Gizzard* is not known for sure. One story says the name originated from an iron-smelting furnace used by the Tennessee Coal and Railroad Co. to test the quality of its coke in the 1870s. Another tale says Davy Crockett burned his tongue on a hot turkey gizzard while camped along the creek. Still others say the name arose during a peace conference when an Indian chief ripped the gizzard from a recently gutted turkey and threw it into the campfire to get the whites' attention. However the name came about, it's now firmly attached to the creeks and the gorge they flow through, Gizzard Cove.

Trailhead: From the SCRA Visitor Center, head east on US 41 and at 2.3 miles turn right at the Grundy Forest State Natural Area sign. Follow the signs through two more right turns. Passing overflow parking on the right,

Blue Hole on Little Fiery Gizzard Creek

continue straight ahead to enter the natural area and park at the picnic area at 3.1 miles.

Description: Begin the day loop to the right of the picnic shelter (built by the CCC in the 1930s). The trail enters the woods; follow the white blazes.

At 0.1 mile, walk over sheets of smooth sandstone along a sandy path to School Branch, which falls 20 feet over a ledge to your left. Here is an arch in formation. The stream flows through a crack in the sandstone along the bluff's edge at the lip of the waterfall, gradually separating a strip of rock from the bluff that could remain as a natural arch.

Following the trail lined with partridgeberry, cross a marshy area on a boardwalk at 0.2 mile. The trail later crosses an old road and a small stream (dry most times of the year) and then swings by the top of a low rock bluff. At 0.6 mile watch for a sinkhole on the right and, just after, an old CCC camp road and building foundations off to the right. This is also the location of the CCC Campsite.

The trail begins a drop into the gorge at 0.9 mile. You can usually hear the Big Fiery Gizzard and possibly see the creek through the trees. Switchback down and left to where the trail joins the creek, which dances from rock to rock through a light-filtered canopy of mountain laurel. With the creek now on your right, giant hemlocks lead the way to Hanes Hole Falls at 1.1 miles; the creek falls over a ragged rock shelf and slips from pool to pool downstream. From here the trail is rocky and narrow, with a steep bank down to the stream on the right.

At 1.2 miles you'll overlook the junction of the Big and Little Fiery Gizzard Creeks. Together they rush and swirl among boulders and rock shelves and escape out of sight into the gorge. The waters of these creeks flow southeast down the plateau to eventually join Battle Creek and then the Tennessee River.

From the confluence, the trail follows the Little Fiery Gizzard Creek upstream to a bridge on the right at 1.3 miles that signals the beginning of the Fiery Gizzard Trail. (The 11.8-mile trail, Hike 2, ends at Foster Falls to the southeast.)

Continue straight ahead to complete the Grundy Forest Day Loop. Watch for the piers of a bridge that once spanned the creek. At 1.5 miles, mount the foundation of an old CCC pump house on the trail's right to view Blue Hole Falls, a 9-foot-high waterfall with an inviting swimming hole below. The trail then crosses the rocky path of School Branch, which you crossed above.

Begin the gradual climb out of the gorge. At 1.8 miles stands Cave Spring Rockhouse, a rock shelter named for the emerging spring; notice the large hemlock nearby. Continue your ascent, switching back left to the blufftop. Atop the bluff, you'll overlook the forest understory from the roof of the rockhouse at 1.9 miles. From there it's a short walk back to the picnic area to close the loop.

2 | FIERY GIZZARD TRAIL

Distance: 12.5 miles one way (Chimney Rocks 1.2 mile one way; Sycamore Falls 1.3 mile one way; Raven Point Campsite 4.5 miles one way; Small Wild Camping Area 9.6 miles one way)
Difficulty: Strenuous
Elevation Gain: 600 ft
Cautions: Boulder fields, stream and fence crossings, steep ascents and descents
Connections: Grundy Forest Day Loop, Dog Hole Trail, Raven Point Trail, Foster Falls/Climbers Loop

Attractions: The Fiery Gizzard Trail is one of the more interesting and challenging trails in the Southeast. Along the way, Big Fiery Gizzard Creek pours through the slot of Black Canyon, the pillars of Chimney Rocks loom in the forest, the creek spills over Sycamore Falls, and numerous overlooks offer views of Gizzard Cove. But while enjoying these sites, you must descend into Gizzard Cove and for much of the first half of the trip step from rock to rock in the boulder-strewn gorge. Then a steep climb takes you out of Gizzard Cove; the trail then follows the rim of the gorge, only to make a precipitous descent into Laurel Gorge and a steep ascent back to the plateautop before continuing to the trail's end at Foster Falls. The difficulty of the trail and its many attractions make this one of the best trails in the region for experienced hikers. Camping is available at the Raven Point Campsite, Small Wild Camping Area, and Father Adamz Campsite and at the end of the trail at Foster Falls TVA Small Wild Area.

Trailhead: From the SCRA Visitor Center, head east on US 41 and at 2.3 miles turn right at

Black Canyon

the Grundy Forest State Natural Area sign. Follow the signs through two more right turns. Passing overflow parking on the right, continue straight ahead to enter the natural area and park at the picnic area at 3.1 miles to pick up the Grundy Forest Day Loop (Hike 1).

Description: Access the Fiery Gizzard Trail by hiking the Grundy Forest Day Loop in either direction. For the shortest access, walk the loop clockwise to the left of the picnic shelter. The trail reaches the top of a bluff with a view into the cove of Little Fiery Gizzard Creek at 0.1 mile and then switchbacks down into the cove. Turn downstream along the creek; Cave Spring Rockhouse opens in the rock bluff on the right. Pass Blue Hole Falls at 0.5 mile and reach a junction with the Fiery Gizzard Trail on the left at 0.7 mile.

Turn left and cross the bridge over Little Fiery Gizzard Creek. On the other side, turn right and, at 0.9 mile, reach the confluence of Big and Little Fiery Gizzard Creeks. The trail then follows the main creek left. Just beyond this junction of creeks, the combined waters pour through a deep rock slot called Black Canyon.

The trail continues downstream along Big Fiery Gizzard Creek, which contains numerous shelves of spilling water. Cross a boulder field, the first of many that make the hiking difficult. At 1.2 miles, Chimney Rocks, pillars of friable rock, stand to the right. Beyond, at 1.3 miles, the trail reaches a junction with a side path 100 yards to 12-foot-high Sycamore Falls on Big Fiery Gizzard Creek. Also notice the tall cascade that pours down the bluff on the far side of the creek; it disappears in dry weather.

Continuing on the main trail, cross an open strip where a gas pipeline has been laid. Then at 1.5 miles is a junction with the 2.8-mile Dog Hole Trail on the left. (The Dog Hole Trail and this section of the Fiery Gizzard form a loop to Raven Point and back for a total hike of 8.8 miles from the Grundy Forest Trailhead.) Continue straight on the Fiery Gizzard Trail.

Soon you'll notice in the dry weather of late summer and early fall that the creek disappears. The water sinks into the creekbed to flow beneath the rocks. At 2.0 miles, the trail descends a stone stairway through the Fruit Bowl, a pile of large boulders. Just beyond the boulder field, the trail leaves Grundy Forest and enters private property; the trail passes through this property by conservation easement.

At 2.2 miles the trail ascends a slope where an old road continues up to the left and the trail stays straight to then descend back to creek level. At 2.6 miles a low, straight ledge in the creek creates a small waterfall. Soon after, another old road comes down from the left; follow the road to the right.

The trail turns up steeply several times and descends back to the bottomland to sometimes rejoin the faint path of the old road and to skirt the edge of the creek. Keep an eye on the white blazes; it's sometimes easy to get off the trail.

At 3.7 miles, the trail begins to make the ascent out of the gorge. The

Chimney Rocks

way becomes steep with switchbacks. As you near the top, watch for a large outcrop of rock to the left and then pass below Raven Point Arch, which you can see if the leaves are off the trees.

Top out at 4.4 miles at a junction with the 0.4-mile side trail to Raven Point, which presents a panoramic view of Gizzard Cove. A few feet after turning right on the side trail, watch to the right for a path to Raven Point Arch, a small span of rock at the edge of the gorge.

At the junction, turn left to stay on the main trail. At 4.5 miles is an intersection. To the left is the other end of the Dog Hole Trail (Hike 3). Straight, a short trail leads to the Raven Point Campsite; water is available from Anderson Creek farther down the main trail, which turns to the right.

A wooden stile helps you over a fence at 4.7 miles. The main trail then turns right while access for Raven Point is to the left across the Baggenstoss Farm; you can walk out to a road in 0.1 mile (see Hike 4).

The Fiery Gizzard Trail wanders through the woods to drop into a small gorge and pass downstream to a ford of Anderson Creek, also called McAlloyd Branch, at 4.9 miles. You'll hear Anderson Falls to the right. You can make your way downstream to the top of the falls, but there's no good view. It's possible to follow a path up to the right and around left to then slip and slide down the steep slope to the bottom; this is difficult, so only experienced outdoorspeople should attempt it. At the bottom, you'll see the falls drop in two steps, about 60 feet in the main fall and then downstream several yards another 20 feet.

Back on the main trail, climb from the creek through boulders and up a low ledge to gain the top of the plateau once again. Skirt the back end of a field on the left; to the right is McAlloyd Cove. At 5.1 miles is a stile left from when a fence, now gone, blocked the way.

The trail curves left up another side gorge to then descend to a ford of Perpendicular Creek at 5.5 miles. Cross another fence stile and turn right, dip to cross a small creekbed, and reach a left turn in the main trail at 5.7 miles, with a side path right that leads to Hemlock View of Raven Point. Turn left.

Through the woods, paralleling Gizzard Cove now, the trail crosses dirt roads at 5.9 and 6.3 miles. You'll then encounter the remains of vats from a moonshine still and follow a stream up to a low overhang at 6.5 miles where the still operated; the stream forms a small waterfall where it drops over the ledge of the overhang. The trail crosses the stream at the base of the falls, turning right.

Continue to parallel Gizzard Cove, passing through secondary forest with occasional dips into low areas and crossings of old roads. After passing an open area that may once have been a field, begin the steep descent into Laurel Gorge at 9.7 miles. When you descend to the first level, turn left and work your way through boulders and then descend along a boulder slope to bottom out and ford Laurel Branch at 9.9 miles; most times you'll be able to rockhop. Then begin a steep ascent of the other side of the gorge with some switchbacks. When you finally regain the rim, turn right to skirt the edge of the gorge and enter the Little Gizzard Creek TVA Small Wild Area. At 10.1 miles, the trail reaches Laurel Gorge Overlook to the right.

Cross Small Wild Branch at 10.2 miles and at a junction keep right along the bluff (straight is the way campers from the TVA Small Wild Camping Area come down to the branch to get water). At 10.3 miles is the entrance to the primitive campsite on the left. Soon after, a path to the right leads to the Small Wild Overlook.

Continuing on the main trail, cross the TVA boundary at 10.4 miles, leaving the Small Wild Camping Area, and then at 10.7 miles cross a stream with a pool above and a view of the rock wall of the gorge to the right. At 11.2 miles, the trail reaches Saddle Horn Rock Overlook. Soon after, the trail dips to cross a small stream.

The trail eventually widens into an old road. At 11.6 miles, there's another old road to the left, but stay straight. The trail dips through a drainage and, at 11.8 miles, reaches Lichen Rock Overlook to the right, which offers a view of Little Gizzard Creek Gorge, a tributary of Gizzard Cove. Cross a boardwalk over a low area and cross the boundary into TVA land that makes up the Foster Falls TVA Small Wild Area.

The trail now turns up Little Gizzard Creek Gorge. At 11.9 miles, a trail to the right is Exit 2 from the Climbers Loop in the gorge (Hike 5). Stay straight to complete the Fiery Gizzard Trail. At 12.0 miles, another path to the right is Exit 1 from the Climbers Loop. Cross three boardwalks over low areas, and soon a path to the left leads to the Father Adamz Campsite, named for an Episcopal priest who served Tracy City and Sewanee in the 1930s–1950s and who was also a naturalist and a scout leader for the children of Tracy City. The main trail reaches the edge of the gorge at an overlook of 60-foot Foster Falls and its deep plunge basin; use caution here because the rock slopes down and there is no railing.

The trail passes a Boy Scout Camp to the left at 12.1 miles and then passes another trail into the Father Adamz Campsite. The trail then turns down right to a steel bridge crossing of Little Gizzard Creek at 12.3 miles; the only water source for the campsites is here. On the other side, a wooden stairway ascends from the bridge, and the trail continues up to the top of the Foster Falls basin. The trail passes by a stone wall that provides an overlook of the top of the falls at 12.4 miles. The trail soon turns left to pass under a powerline into the woods and crosses a bridge over a small stream to reach the picnic area, end of the trail, and parking for Foster Falls at 12.5 miles.

3 | DOG HOLE TRAIL

Distance: 2.8 miles one way
Difficulty: Moderate
Elevation Gain: 200 ft
Cautions: Stream crossings, steep descent
Connections: Fiery Gizzard Trail, Raven Point Trail

Attractions: This trail creates an 8.8-mile loop with the Grundy Forest Day Loop and the Fiery Gizzard Trail, offering great views along the way, including Werner Point Overlook. The Werner family operated the Werner Lumber company, which began in the late 1880s and closed in 1942; the family still owns much of the land in the region.

The Dog Hole Mine, for which the trail is named, is a low opening in the wall of Gizzard Cove. Such coal mines were called dog hole mines because only a dog could stand upright in the short space. Camping is available at the Raven Point Campsite.

Trailhead: From the SCRA Visitor Center, head east on US 41 and at 2.3 miles turn right at the Grundy Forest State Natural Area sign. Follow the signs through two more right turns. Passing overflow parking on the right, continue straight ahead to enter the natural area and park at the picnic area at 3.1 miles. Walk 0.7 mile along the Grundy Forest Day Loop (Hike 1) clockwise and then 0.8 mile along the Fiery Gizzard Trail (Hike 2) to reach the beginning of the Dog Hole Trail. Because the Fiery Gizzard and Dog Hole Trails make a good day loop from here, and it's best to first hike the difficult Fiery Gizzard Trail to Raven Point and then use the Dog Hole Trail to return to this point, this description of the Dog Hole Trail starts at the Raven Point end. Continue straight on the Fiery Gizzard Trail to Raven Point and turn left to the Raven Point Campsite, where you'll find the junction with the other end of the Dog Hole Trail; so far you will have walked 4.5 miles. (A shorter access to this point is detailed in the description of Hike 4; you will need a car shuttle if you intend to walk the Dog Hole Trail one way.)

Description: Following the Dog Hole Trail from the junction at the Raven Point Campsite, wander through the plateau forest along the rim of Gizzard Cove. The trail passes through a number of swales, broad depressions hollowed out by draining water that seem to draw you down into the gorge.

At 0.2 mile, the trail dips to cross a small creek, dry much of the year. At 0.3 mile is a rock overlook of Gizzard Cove and then two more beyond that are collectively called Flat Rock Overlooks. To the left from these overlooks, you'll see the ridge leading out to Raven Point.

Continuing on the trail, dip to cross another small creek, dry in late summer and fall, and reach a side trail on the left to Werner Point Overlook at 0.9 mile. This side path leads 150 yards out to one of the best overlooks of the gorge.

The main trail leads along a rock bluff at 1.2 miles where old cars have been pushed over and abandoned. You'll come upon a stone passageway that was the walls of the potato house on the old Sam Werner Farm; this is private property, so do not trespass.

The trail continues to swing along rock bluffs and then descends through a field of mountain laurel to cross a small stream, dry sometimes, to a junction at 1.6 miles. A path to the right leads 80 yards up to Yellow Pine Falls, a small waterfall in a rock alcove.

Continuing on the main trail, cross a small streambed, descend a low ledge, dip through several more small streambeds (dry much of the time), and then cross a cleared strip in the forest at 2.5 miles where a gas pipeline has been laid. The trail then skirts a fence line and descends to turn left and begin a steep descent into the gorge. Cross the pipeline path again and drop below a rock bluff.

At 2.7 miles, in the base of the rock wall on the left, is the old coal mine from which the trail gets its name. From the mine, stay along the base of the rock wall and then turn down right to reach the junction with the Fiery Gizzard Trail at 2.8 miles. It's then 1.5 miles back to the Grundy Forest trailhead to complete the 8.8-mile loop, or 4.3 miles total for a one-way hike between Raven Point and Grundy Forest.

4 | RAVEN POINT TRAIL

Distance: 0.8 mile one way
Difficulty: Easy
Elevation Change: Level
Cautions: Fence stiles, pasture crossing, high bluff
Connections: Fiery Gizzard Trail, Dog Hole Trail

Attractions: With 200-foot cliffs, Raven Point thrusts into the gorge, offering a panoramic view of Gizzard Cove. This route is a short alternative to hiking the Fiery Gizzard Trail to access Raven Point. Camping is available at the Raven Point Campsite.

  Trailhead: From the SCRA Visitor Center, turn east on US 41. In Tracy City, at 3.2 miles, turn right, still on US 41. Pass the Dutch Maid Bakery, where hikers traditionally stop to sample the baked goods. Turn right again at 3.4 miles on the small road beside Don's Drugs. At 4.5 miles stay straight at a fork. The road curves sharply to the right at 5.6 miles and then curves back left. At 6.0 miles, turn right into the driveway past a white house, the home of one of the Baggenstoss brothers. Pull over to the left and park. You'll see a sign welcoming hikers; there is no overnight parking. Please stay on the trail and respect private property.

Raven Point

Description: Climb over the fence stile where you see a sign for the Fiery Gizzard Trail. Step over a small stream, and then follow the path skirting the edge of the pasture to another fence stile just in the woods on your left at 0.1 mile. Here you join the Fiery Gizzard Trail (Hike 2). Turn right to climb over the stile and follow the trail to a junction at 0.3 mile. Raven Point Campsite lies to your right. The Dog Hole Trail (Hike 3) leads straight ahead. Turn left to head toward Raven Point.

At 0.4 mile the Fiery Gizzard Trail turns off to the right and drops into Gizzard Cove. Stay straight here, now following blue blazes. Soon a faint side path leads right a short distance to Raven Point Arch, a span of 12 feet with a clearance of 6 feet.

Foster Falls

Continue on the main trail along the narrowing ridge to Raven Point at 0.8 mile. Birds of prey soaring on the updrafts from the depths of the gorge are a common sight. The bluff faces west, offering a spectacular sunset view.

5 FOSTER FALLS / CLIMBERS LOOP

Distance: 2.0-mile loop (Foster Falls 0.4 mile one way)
Difficulty: Strenuous
Elevation Change: 150 ft
Cautions: Steep descent and ascent, rocky path
Connections: Fiery Gizzard Trail

Attractions: This trail leads down to the base of 60-foot Foster Falls in a steep-walled gorge and then continues west, providing access to the gorge wall for rock climbers before connecting with the Fiery Gizzard Trail. Camping is available at the Father Adamz Campsite (on the Fiery Gizzard Trail) and at the Foster Falls TVA Small Wild Area.

When conservationists were trying to get the SCRA established, they enticed the TVA, the giant federal utility that serves the Tennessee River Valley, to help with the project. TVA helped plan the recreation area, donated money toward its development, and established the Foster Falls TVA Small Wild Area, which it manages jointly with the Tennessee Division of State Parks. The campground near the picnic area has running water and hot showers. Camping here is first-come, first-served, with a fee. The campground is closed in late fall and winter; check with the SCRA Visitor Center for the dates.

Trailhead: From the SCRA Visitor Center, head east on US 41. At 3.2 miles in Tracy City, turn right and continue on US 41. At 11.0 miles, turn right into Foster Falls TVA Small Wild Area and park at the picnic area at 11.5 miles.

Description: Begin your hike from the picnic area at the sign for Foster Falls. The trail leads across a bridge over a small stream and under a powerline to the bluff above Little Gizzard Creek Gorge. Cables line the edge. Along the bluff to the right, the path joins the lower end of the Fiery Gizzard Trail (Hike 2). To hike to the bottom of Foster Falls, turn left and walk along the bluff. At 0.1 mile, a stone wall overlook offers a grand view of Little Gizzard Creek as it drops 60 feet to form Foster Falls, seated in a 120-foot sandstone plunge basin.

From the overlook, turn back out to the powerline and walk down the clearing; a trail to the left connects with the campground. At 0.2 mile turn right, back into the woods, and descend a stairway to then curve left below the rimrock of the gorge. The trail soon turns down right to make a winding, steep, rocky descent into the gorge. At the bottom at 0.4 mile, a suspension bridge carries you over Little Gizzard Creek. On the other side, turn right to get to the plunge pool at the foot of Foster Falls, the area's highest-volume waterfall. The rock walls of the basin tower over the pool, which has become a favorite swimming hole for campers.

You can retrace your path from here if you are only after a good view of the falls or a swim. But to complete this loop hike, turn left after crossing the bridge to walk along the foot of the rock bluff. This is a popular area for rock climbers; the trail was constructed primarily to provide access to good climbing walls, but the trail makes a nice hike as well, providing close-up views of the vertical sandstone bluffs.

Ascend stone steps to the foot of the rock wall and continue west along the escarpment. Occasionally, large blocks of stone that have fallen from the rim sit on the left .

At 1.0 mile, the trail forks, with the right-hand path providing the first exit out of the gorge. To stay on the main trail, turn down left.

A side trail to the right at 1.1 miles simply provides access to a climbing spot; there is no hiking exit here. Continue straight. Other side trails may develop as climbers access the rock wall; just stay with the blazed trail.

At 1.4 miles is another fork with Exit 2 up to the right. The trail continues left along the rock bluff, providing more access for rock climbs, but the path eventually disappears among the boulders at the foot of the wall. To complete the loop, turn right up Exit 2, climb steeply, and turn to the left to a wooden stairway that ascends the rock lip at the gorge rim. Now on top of the bluff, the trail wanders through the woods to connect with the Fiery Gizzard Trail at 1.5 miles. Turn right.

Pass the junction where Exit 1 emerges from the gorge and pass the Father Adamz Campsite and an overlook of Foster Falls. Turn down right to cross Little Gizzard Creek on a metal bridge and walk along the rock bluff above Foster Falls. Past the falls, bear left to cross under a powerline and over a footbridge spanning a small stream, and emerge behind the picnic shelter at the parking area at 2.1 miles.

6 | LONE ROCK LOOP

Distance: 1.5-mile loop
Difficulty: Easy
Elevation Change: 50 ft
Cautions: Steps
Connections: None

Attractions: The trail circles the largest of the four lakes at Grundy Lakes State Park and loops by remains of the Lone Rock Mine Coke Ovens built in 1883.

One of the Lone Rock Mine Coke Ovens

Grundy Lake and Lone Rock Lake were here during the early coal-mining days. The CCC stabilized these lakes and created two smaller ones in the 1930s. Herman Baggenstoss, one of the sons of the bakery family, was with the U.S. Forest Service at the time and served as project supervisor. Later, as Grundy County Conservation Board chair, he was one of the main forces behind the establishment of the SCRA; a plaque honoring him is mounted on the wall at the entrance to the SCRA Visitor Center.

Earthen banks around the lake contain the coke ovens. For many years in the late 1800s, convicts leased from the state worked these coke ovens and the nearby Lone Rock coal mines; 130 brick coke ovens at this site were used to heat coal and transform it into coke, which can be used as a fuel in industrial processes because it burns hotter than coal.

Trailhead: From the SCRA Visitor Center, turn east on US 41. In Tracy City, at 3.2 miles, turn right, still on US 41. Beyond Tracy City, watch for a sign at 4.0 miles that directs you left to Grundy Lakes. At 4.6 miles, enter Grundy Lakes State Park and follow the shore of Grundy Lake, the largest of the lakes, on your left. Coke-oven remains line the road on your right. At 4.9 miles, turn left down into the parking area beside the lake.

Description: At the far end of the parking area, walk up the small exit road and turn off left to a bridge crossing of a small creek to begin the loop; the return will be down this road from across the highway. On the other side of the creek, a path to the right leads 0.1 mile up to a loop road that runs around the lake area. Stay left on the main trail, which skirts Grundy Lake to the right.

At 0.4 mile, the trail turns away from the lake to ascend, passing over a small bridge and up steps, to the top of an earthen dam holding the upper Lone Rock Lake.

Cross the dam to your left; then turn left again down wooden steps alongside the Lone Rock Lake spillway. Cross a wooden bridge to the right at 0.6 mile. Skirt Grundy Lake on your left until the trail comes out to a road leading to a lake-point picnic table. Turn left on the road, and then right at the picnic area, back into the woods.

Stone steps lead right over a rock wall at 0.7 mile. Bear left between earthen banks that contain coke ovens. You can make your way left around to the front of the ovens (a path right leads up to a picnic area and exercise course). Stay straight on the main trail, which drops to the lake's edge and continues around Grundy Lake.

At 1.0 mile, cross a footbridge and climb steps up the bank to the paved road that circles the lakes. Turn left on the road and cross the dam that backs up Grundy Lake.

After reaching the highway at 1.1 miles, turn left. The trail soon turns right off the road into the woods and then left, paralleling the road between rows of coke ovens. At 1.2 miles, the trail forks, with the right fork ascending above the road and the ovens and finally descending and stepping down wooden stairs to a clearing beside the highway at 1.4 miles. The left fork continues straight ahead, passing behind the row of coke ovens on the left and a rock wall on the right, crossing a boardwalk over a low area, and emerging in the open beside the highway where the two forks come back together. From here, turn left to cross the highway. Before you cross the highway, you'll see another path to the right, not used as often and so a little overgrown, that leads 0.1 mile up to a parking area near the two smaller lakes: the lower Grassy Lake and the upper Old Muddy Lake. To complete the loop, walk across the highway onto the small road leading down to the parking area beside Grundy Lake. Close the loop at the bridge crossing to the right and return to your vehicle.

7 | BUGGYTOP TRAIL AND SEWANEE NATURAL BRIDGE

Distance: 2.2 miles one way
Difficulty: Moderate
Elevation Loss: 600 ft
Cautions: Rough footing, high bluffs, steep descent
Connections: None

Attractions: Lost Cove Cave's Buggytop Entrance is one of the plateau's most impressive cave entrances, an 80-foot mouth carved out of a 150-foot cliff. On the way to the Buggytop trailhead, stop at the largest-known natural bridge on the South Cumberland.

Trailhead: At 5.7 miles west of I-24 on US 64/41A, after passing the community of Sewanee, turn south on TN 56. At 8.0 miles a side road left off TN 56 leads to the Sewanee Natural Bridge State Natural Area in 2.0 miles. The University of the South donated the bridge, which has a span of 50 feet and a height of 27 feet; from the top, you have a view into Lost Cove. Continuing on TN 56, the highway begins a descent off the edge of the plateau. Find parking on the left for Carter State Natural Area, 12.3 miles from the interstate.

Description: From the parking area, take the Buggytop Trail through limestone boulders up Spur Ridge. The way can be quite muddy in winter. At 0.2 mile, notice a large sinkhole on the right, just as the trail levels out and swings left. In reaching this natural area, you dropped off the plateau and descended into a region of exposed limestone where caves and sinks form.

From the sinkhole, follow the ridgeline north to pass over the highest point of the trail and arrive at a day hiker signup stand at 0.7 mile. A path left here leads 100 yards out to TN 56 about half a mile up from the parking area. The main trail descends from the signup stand. Walk through a forest rich with wildflowers in spring and summer, including the rare Gattinger's rosinweed, also called Cumberland rosinweed; the 6- to 8-foot plant blooms yellow in August.

At 0.8 mile the trail crosses a normally dry creekbed with sculptured rock outcrops resembling clamshells to your right. Watch for where the trail passes sandstone remnants at 1.0 mile and a sinkhole to the right. On a

Buggytop Entrance to Lost Cove Cave

cold day, warm air drifting from this hole makes a slight vapor trail.

Continue a steady descent. At 1.4 miles the trail crosses the boundary into the state natural area, designated by red markings on a large beech tree. The trail to this point crosses private land with an easement. Continue to descend; cross a footbridge over a usually dry streambed at 1.5 miles. Soon after, you may be able to see through trees down the valley to the community of Sherwood to the right. At 1.6 miles, work through rocks and curve left to cross the old Sherwood/Lost Cove Road at 1.7 miles. Just beyond this junction, the trail forks at the top of a bluff, with the Peter Cave Entrance to Lost Cove Cave to the left and the Buggytop Cave Entrance to the right.

First, stay right with the Buggytop Trail along the bluff's edge. Switch left to make a steep climb down to the cave entrance at 2.0 miles. The way can be muddy and slippery in wet weather. In summer, you can feel a cool breeze escaping from the cave mouth. In winter and spring, the emerging Crow Creek can be a torrent of water; far above where it sinks into Lost Cove Cave, the stream is called Lost Creek.

It is possible to follow Crow Creek upstream through the cave past a second entrance on the right, up a sandy bank, and out the Peter Cave Entrance. You must be an experienced caver and have the proper equipment to make the quarter-mile, 2-hour trip. Or check with the SCRA Visitor Center for ranger-guided trips. Do not enter the cave when the creek is up.

From the Buggytop Entrance, retrace your steps back to the junction on the bluff and take the trail left toward the Peter Cave Entrance. The trail passes along the bluff edge over the Buggytop Entrance for a view down Upper Crow Creek Valley. At 0.1 mile along this trail, pass a second cave entrance on your left, probably formed by the collapse of the cave ceiling. Continuing on, you'll reach a normally dry streambed; walk up it a few paces and then turn right uphill to the Peter Cave Entrance at 0.2 mile.

8 | SEWANEE PERIMETER TRAIL

**Distance: 20.0-mile loop (Shakerag Hollow section
    1.4 miles from Greens View to US 64/41A;
    Proctor's Hall 0.6 mile one way from University
    View)**
Difficulty: Moderate
Elevation Change: 300 ft
Cautions: Bluffs, highway crossings, stream crossings
Connections: Bridal Veil Falls Trail

Attractions: This series of connecting paths circles the University of the South at Sewanee, with a number of spectacular views from the western bluff of the plateau. Since the Sewanee Perimeter Trail is on the university domain, public access could be limited or even eliminated at any time in the future. At this writing, the trail may be used by the public for day use only.

Trailhead: Head southwest on US 64/41A from I-24, and after passing through the pillars that mark the entrance to the Domain of the University at 4.0 miles, bear right on University Avenue. Then turn right on Texas Avenue, and in another 0.4 mile turn right on Brakefield Road. Then turn left on Lake Cheston Drive 0.3 mile to parking at the Lake Cheston Recreation Area. (You'll find other access to the Sewanee Perimeter Trail farther down Brakefield Road near the stables, at Greens View at the end

The War Memorial Cross at University View

of Greens View Road, at University View at the end of Tennessee Avenue, and at the west junction of University Avenue and US 64/41A, where the trail passes through the business area. Morgans Steep, at the end of Morgans Steep Road, also offers access, but there's little room for parking.) At the Lake Cheston parking area, walk down a gated dirt road to the left. Descend to cross a small stream and Claras Point Road at 0.2 mile and then continue to a junction with the Sewanee Perimeter Trail at 0.3 mile. To the left on the Sewanee Perimeter Trail is Morgans Steep; turn right to walk the trail clockwise.

Description: The trail crosses a footbridge over Wiggins Creek. You'll see the Bridal Veil Falls Trail (Hike 9) to the left; the main trail is blazed blue, and side trails are blazed white. The Sewanee Perimeter Trail climbs and follows the bluff behind several houses and enters the woods at 0.3 mile. Turn right up to an old road and then left along the road to Oteys View at 0.6 mile (named for Bishop James Harvey Otey, one of the founders and the first chancellor of the university). Watch for where the trail turns down left here. Then skirt the head of a hollow, where the trail crosses a small creek and connects with a road at 0.9 mile. The road right provides 0.3-mile access from the stables area.

Continuing on the trail, cross a small creek and join an old road, but then turn left off the road and left again where a path comes in from the right, and reach the rock outcrop of Elliott Point at 2.4 miles (named for Bishop Stephen Elliott, another founder of the university and the third chancellor).

At 2.6 miles cross an old road and then drop to cross a creekbed and immediately turn left uphill. Soon after, you'll have some good views of Hawkins Cove through the trees. The trail dips through a drainage and then drops to a dirt road; go straight. At 3.3 miles is a junction with another road; turn left to cross an earthen dam forming a lake to your right. Just after crossing the dam, watch for where the trail turns left off the road.

At 4.0 miles the trail reaches the bluff once again, with overlooks across to the War Memorial cross that stands atop University View. (This Polk Lookout is named for Bishop Leonidas Polk, one of the founders and the second chancellor.) At 4.5 miles, intersect with a road and turn right to walk up to the site of Kings Farm at 4.6 miles. Continue straight down the road from the homesite and watch for a left turn on a side road at 4.7 miles. The road descends toward the bluff and levels out at 5.2 miles, where another

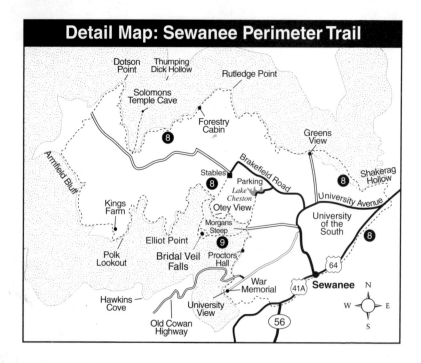

Detail Map: Sewanee Perimeter Trail

road comes down from the right, and then curves right as it follows the bluff around. Stay with the road until the trail turns right and ascends the slope at 5.7 miles to then pass along Armfield Bluff (named for Colonel John Armfield, one of the first trustees of the university, who hosted planning sessions at Beersheba Springs as early as 1857).

After a couple of footbridge crossings of creeks, ascend to a right turn on the trace of an old road at 6.4 miles. The trail crosses another creekbed and reaches an intersection of roads at 6.7 miles; stay straight. The trail turns left at 6.8 miles and meets a more obvious road and turns right at 6.9 miles. At 7.1 miles, intersect with Brakefield Road. The trail used to turn right, but a newer section of trail has been opened to Dotson Point. So turn left and then right down a gated side road, which leads out a point of land. At 7.8 miles is a junction with the main trail right and a path straight leading 0.1 mile out to Dotson Point (named for a local family); stand on the block of stone at the point for a grand view north.

Back on the main trail, cross a couple of streams on footbridges and reach a bluff above Dick Creek at 9.1 miles. Bear right, then turn left and cross the stream on a footbridge. The trail swings near Brakefield Road and then at 9.3 miles reaches a side road. To the right a gate blocks vehicle access off Brakefield Road. Left down the road takes you into Thumping Dick Hollow to Solomons Temple Cave. Only experienced outdoorspeople should attempt to find the cave. (A half mile down the road is a collapsed bridge at a stream crossing. On the other side, turn left off the road, following a faint path downstream until you reach an overhang on the left side of the creek, then bear right away from the creek around to the cave. A small opening to the right leads up to a 30-foot chimney, a hole up through the rock; just beyond, the cave opens on two levels in a sinkhole with a stream flowing out of the lower one. Do not enter the cave or the chimney.)

On the main trail, cross the road leading into Thumping Dick Hollow and continue through the woods. Skirt the bluff above the hollow, cross an old road and a stream, and join an old road to the left to eventually intersect with a gravel road at 10.9 miles. Turn left and stay with the main road as it curves right. Drop to cross an earthen dam holding back a lake and walk up to the university's forestry cabin at 11.1 miles. Past the cabin, the trail bears left off the road and then swings right to parallel the bluff once again.

The trail drops to cross a small stream, where a road comes down from the right, and then at 11.5 miles swings around Rutledge Point (named for Arthur Middleton Rutledge, a trustee instrumental in obtaining land for the university domain). Soon after, connect with an old road that leads out to Brakefield Road in about a mile (at an intersection you'd take the second left).

Continuing on the main trail, connect with the end of a road at 12.8 miles that leads to the right half a mile to Brakefield Road, near the stables. Left on this road a short distance and then right on a path will take you out to a good view at Fraternity Point.

The trail descends into a hollow at 13.4 miles and bears left down an old road to eventually emerge onto paved Alto Road at 13.7 miles. Turn right, walk up the road, and watch for where the trail turns left off the road at 13.8 miles.

Back in the woods, cross a footbridge over a streambed and pass an old car abandoned in the woods. Then watch for a double blaze that signals a turn down left through blocks of stone and then right. At 14.2 miles is an intersection with a side trail that leads up to Greens View, providing access. (Some sections of this side trail are steep as it works its way left up a drainage area through boulders and then right to emerge at the parking area in 0.2 mile.)

The main trail continues below the bluff through an area known for its wildflowers. At 15.2 miles, the trail drops to cross a stream on two footbridges and soon after begins a steep uphill climb. There's a junction with an old road at 15.4 miles. To the right was the Sewanee Mining Company's first commercial coal mine, Sewanee 1, which because of the low yield was mined for only a short time before the mining operations were moved to Tracy City.

Turn left along the road to stay on the trail and soon curve right as you ascend Shakerag Hollow. (People wanting to buy moonshine waved a rag above their heads when entering the hollow to assure the moonshiners of their good intentions.) You'll soon reach the head of the hollow, marked by a small waterfall. The trail turns right off the old road and then intersects with another old road; turn left and walk out to US 64/41A at the pillars marking the entrance to the university domain at 15.6 miles.

The trail now crosses the highway and enters a pine woods. At 15.7 miles, drop onto the bed of the old rail spur that was built from the main rail line at Cowan up the plateau during the coal mining years. The route was so steep, the spur was called the Mountain Goat. The rail line was abandoned in 1985, and now the railbed has been proposed as a bike path. Turn right and walk down the old railbed, which can be muddy.

Cross three roads and enter the business district of Sewanee at 17.1 miles. Pass right in front of the pharmacy and market; across the highway stands Shenanigans Restaurant. Keep on the railbed, the tread nearest the highway. At 17.7 miles, cross TN 56 and continue down the railbed to turn off right at 17.9 miles and cross US 64/41A.

The trail reenters the woods. At 18.7 miles, climb steeply to pass under a powerline and then connect with an old road at a barrier blocking vehicle access at University View; the large cross is a memorial to those from the University, Sewanee, and Franklin County who died in wars. Follow the road around in front of the cross and turn left beside a stone bench.

(This next section of trail was called the Corso and was built in the 1930s by the CCC. The CCC also constructed the section of trail through Shakerag Hollow and the trail beyond Morgans Steep, which was called the Arcadian. The remainder of the Sewanee Perimeter Trail was completed in 1992.)

At 19.1 miles the trail descends to cross a stream and join an old road. Turn left on the road, which is the old Cowan Highway. Curve right off the road as it curves left. The path now passes below the rock bluff of the plateau rim. Curve behind a waterfall and pass under a long overhang to reach Proctors Hall at 19.4 miles. Before entering this rock tunnel, formed by a large slab of rock spanning a gap between boulders, you can follow a path up to the right that takes you on top for a view; a path up behind the rock leads out to Proctors Hall Road.

Pass through Proctors Hall (be careful climbing down the rock on the other side) then pass under another overhang. At 19.6 miles, the trail bears left down toward a creek, descending some steps. But before reaching the creek, where there is a small waterfall, the trail turns right upstream. The trail narrows along a rock wall, crosses a side stream, and then crosses the main stream at 19.7 miles and turns left downstream. The trail swings right to ascend steps to reach Morgans Steep at 19.8 miles (named for Judge Oliver J. Morgan, who made a donation to complete the endowment for the university in 1859). Continue along the bluff and then drop into a hollow to the junction at Wiggins Creek at 20.0 miles, which closes the loop. The trail up to the right leads back to Lake Cheston.

9 | BRIDAL VEIL FALLS TRAIL

Distance: 1.5 miles one way (Bridal Veil Falls 0.9 mile one way)
Difficulty: Moderate
Elevation Loss: 400 ft
Cautions: Stream crossings, rough footing
Connections: Sewanee Perimeter Trail

Attractions: Along this trail, laced with wildflowers in spring, a stream emerges from the mountainside, cascades delicately, and drops into a dramatic limestone pit. Since the Bridal Veil Falls Trail is on the university domain, public access could be limited or even eliminated at any time in the future. At this writing, the trail may be used by the public for day use only.

Trailhead: Head southwest on US 64/41A from I-24, and after passing through the pillars that mark the entrance to the Domain of the University at 4.0 miles, bear right on University Avenue. Then turn right on Texas Avenue, and in another 0.4 mile turn right on Brakefield Road. Then turn left on Lake Cheston Drive 0.3 mile to parking at the Lake Cheston Recreation Area. Hike down the old road to make the connection with the Sewanee

Bridal Veil Falls (photo by Sondra Jamieson)

Perimeter Trail (Hike 8) in 0.3 mile and turn right across the creek to the Bridal Veil Falls Trail junction on the left. From this point you can walk a 2.4-mile loop using this trail and a 0.9-mile section of the Sewanee Perimeter Trail.

Description: Descend below the bluff on a path that has running water in wet weather and watch for a waterfall up to the right after recent rains. Passing through scattered boulders, the trail levels out in a forest of mixed hardwoods and then descends to a junction at 0.8 mile. The loop trail follows an old road north, to the right, but before heading that way, turn left for the easier descent to the waterfall or keep straight for the more difficult descent.

Going straight, descend to a layered rock balanced on the edge of a large sinkhole that contains the waterfall. To the right of the rock, descend steeply to climb down a muddy path and circle to stand in front of Bridal Veil Falls. Veils of water delicately shower 25 feet over a layered wall then plunge another 25 feet into a limestone pit.

Facing the falls, you can return to the trail junction by taking the path to the right that circles back above the falls; watch for a side path to the right as you climb up from the falls that leads along the ridge to the vertical shaft of Kirby Cave, one of several small caves once part of a large cave system connected to the sinkhole at Bridal Veil Falls. Do not enter these caves.

Back at the trail junction above the falls, you can retrace your steps back to Lake Cheston if you only want to see the waterfall. Or you can continue the loop hike by taking the old road north. The road curves right to a junction with another old road at 0.9 mile. The hike turns right at this junction, but first turn left a short distance to Olivers Rock, a large boulder resting in the forest. This road left circles the rock to descend to another cascading stream that ends in a sinkhole, at 0.1 mile from the junction; there's also a larger stream, Pinckney Branch, to the left.

Return to the junction and continue straight up the road (or turn right if you did not walk to Olivers Rock). The road curves left as it ascends the slope, eventually leading below the bluff once again. Bear right up a cove with a creek to the left, a tributary of Pinckney Branch. The trail crosses the creek and then curves right and ascends to join the Sewanee Perimeter Trail at 1.5 miles at a junction below the university stables. It's 0.3 mile straight up a road to the stables if you have a car shuttle waiting for you, or you can turn right on the Sewanee Perimeter Trail and return to the beginning of the Bridal Veil Falls Trail in 0.9 mile.

10 | FRANKLIN STATE FOREST TRAILS

Distance: 11.1 miles one way (Tom Pack Falls Loop 1.5 miles; Sweden Cove Trail 1.3 miles one way; North Rim Trail to Collins Falls 2.9 miles one way; West Rim Trail 5.4 miles one way)
Difficulty: Moderate
Elevation Change: 150 ft
Cautions: Creek crossings, boulder hopping
Connections: None

Attractions: Franklin State Forest was established in 1936 from 6,941 acres purchased from the Cross Creek Coal Company, which operated in the

South Cumberland region. Soon after, the CCC entered the area to construct buildings and trails.

Located near the SCRA and the University of the South, the state forest offers more hiking opportunities on the South Cumberland. A loop trail passes by Tom Pack Falls, and trails along the rim of Sweden Cove at the edge of the plateau lead to waterfalls and overlooks. Camping is permitted anywhere. Be aware of the hunting seasons.

Trailhead: At 3.2 miles southwest of I-24 on US 64/41A, just before the entrance to the University of the South and across from Saint Andrews School, turn south on TN 156. Stay with TN 156 through a couple of turns 7.7 miles to enter Franklin State Forest, where you'll see the headquarters on the right. Turn in the gravel road and head back 0.1 mile to the end of the gravel and park. If you're hiking the entire trail system, you'll probably want to run a shuttle at the other end of the West Rim Trail at the forest lookout tower that's on TN 156 another 3.8 miles south of the forest headquarters.

Description: Head straight into the woods past the trailhead sign. Walk through a logged area, crossing a creek in the middle, and then bear left down to a junction at 0.4 mile at CCC Lake.

Tom Pack Falls

Overlooking Sweden Cove

At the junction, turn right to walk the loop to Tom Pack Falls. Circle the lake and cross the end of Lake Road at a picnic and camping area; the only water available is from the stream feeding the lake. (Lake Road turns west off TN 156 just south of the forest headquarters.)

As the trail continues, it passes through thick stands of laurel that bloom in April and May. Cross a stream on a bridge at 0.7 mile and later cross a jeep track and then descend to Tom Pack Falls at 1.1 miles. A path leads down and across the creek for a better view of the 20-foot curtain of water.

Continue straight along a rock wall and watch for a turn down left that leads to a bridge crossing of the creek below the falls at 1.2 miles. Then hike up and left to emerge onto Lake Road once again at 1.7 miles. Walk around the lake to reach a junction with the Sweden Cove Trail to the right at 1.9 miles. Straight ahead, you can cross the bridge over the creek to close the loop and hike back to the trailhead if you're only out to see Tom Pack Falls.

The Sweden Cove Trail leads up through the woods to cross Lake Road at 2.2 miles and then descends to cross TN 156 at 2.4 miles. Back into the woods, cross a couple of old road depressions, pass through a couple of low areas, and walk up to a junction at the head of Sweden Cove at 2.8 miles. (The cove in the eastern edge of the Cumberland Plateau is actually misnamed; it should be *Sweeton*, for a family of early settlers.)

The West Rim Trail turns right. But you can first turn left on a 2.9-mile trail branch following the north rim of the cove. Along this North Rim Trail, cross a small stream and pass through more laurel thickets and descend to a path right at 0.3 mile that leads to a scenic overlook. Along this path, cross a small stream and walk out to a rock promontory view of Sweden Cove with a cascading stream down to the left, a tributary of Sweden Creek that drains the cove. Back on the main trail, continue to descend into a low area and then walk up to a right turn in the trail at 0.4 mile. Pass along a bluff and then head up the cascading stream that forms the waterfall you saw from the overlook. The trail leads to a footbridge crossing at 0.6 mile. Turning back downstream and then through the woods, emerge onto the end of an old road at 1.0 mile, where you can walk right to another overlook. The trail crosses the road and descends through the woods to a stream rockhop at 1.3 miles.

Paralleling the edge of the cove, cross more wet-weather streams and reach a grand view at 2.0 miles; here you'll see Collins Cove to the left where it joins Sweden Cove, and you can see down Sweden Cove to where it opens into the valley of Battle Creek that flows southeast to join the Tennessee River. At 2.1 miles, you'll have another panoramic view of the merging coves. The trail descends to cross a stream on a bridge at 2.2 miles. After another view, pass through a wet area to hop over a stream at 2.8 miles. On the other side, the trail stays with the white blazes to the right, not up the more obvious path to the left that leads toward red markings on trees at the boundary of the state forest. The trail drops below the rim of Collins Cove and winds down the rugged slope to end at Collins Falls just outside the forest boundary at 2.9 miles. The stream that drains Collins Cove cascades steeply down the slope to then run through the cove before joining Sweden Creek in Sweden Cove.

Back at the main trail junction with the North Rim Trail left at the head of Sweden Cove, turn south along the west rim of the cove. On this West Rim Trail, drop to rockhop a small stream and then drop into a low area at 2.9 miles from the trailhead, where a path left leads to a precipitous view of a waterfall where the creek spills into the cove. Each of the streams at the head of the cove is a branch of Sweden Creek.

At 3.3 miles, a side path leads straight out to an overlook as the main trail turns down right. This overlook offers the best view down Sweden Cove. Another path left to an overlook at 3.6 miles gives a grudging view of a waterfall to the right. Continuing on the main trail, curve left to cross the creek that feeds the waterfall.

The trail skirts a bluff dropoff and passes through a large cut tree to cross a creek at 4.1 miles. Drop off the bluff to pass by a small overhang with a dripping spring. Cross Pole Bridge Creek at 4.2 miles between the upper and middle falls of a triple-step waterfall. The trail passes through and over boulders and skirts a large overhang before ascending back to the rim. At 4.6 miles, cross a stream and again descend below the bluff and later ascend back to the blufftop to cross an old road and continue left. For a third time, step over a small creek and descend below the bluff at 5.3 miles. The trail crosses a cascading stream on stepping stones and climbs back to the blufftop. Now stay on top for the rest of the hike. At 5.8 miles the trail crosses a stream with a small waterfall to the left at the head of Panther Cove. The trail then curves left to a rock overlook of the falls. At 5.9 miles is a junction; left leads to an old overlook, overgrown unless it has been cleared by the time you get there, and right is an old route where you might see a blaze on a tree, but stay straight.

At 6.4 miles, the trail crosses an old road at a small creek and curves left to parallel Panther Hollow Road. The trail joins the road at 6.6 miles. Walk down the road to where it curves right away from the bluff at 6.9 miles; a path left leads to a nice overlook. Staying with the road as it heads west away from the bluff, ascend the ridge until the trail turns left off the road at 7.7 miles.

The trail then passes through a hollow. At 8.1 miles is Cave Spring, where a rock overhang protects a dripping spring. The trail passes above the cave to connect with an old road. Left is an old homesite. Turn right and walk up the road to the parking area near the forest lookout tower on TN 156 at 8.2 miles from the trailhead. The North Rim Trail to Collins Falls and back adds 5.8 miles to the hike.

Map 2. Savage Gulf State Natural Area

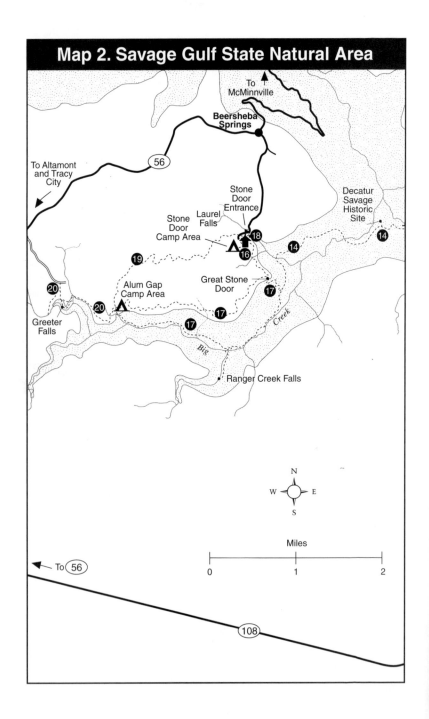

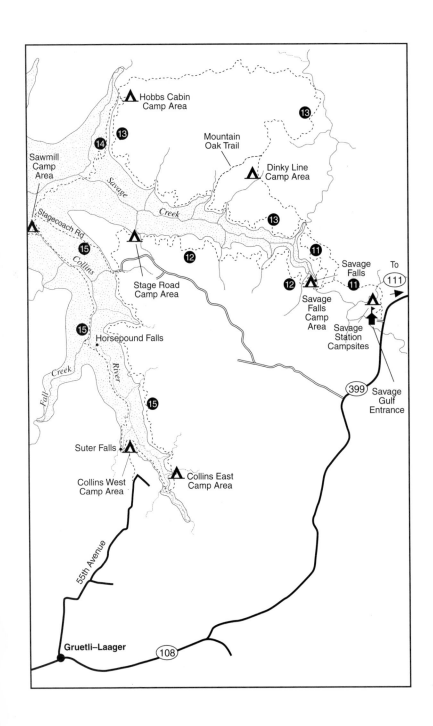

SAVAGE GULF STATE NATURAL AREA

The largest unit of the South Cumberland Recreation Area (SCRA), Savage Gulf State Natural Area encompasses 11,500 acres of some of the most primitive and isolated lands in Tennessee. Three converging gorges, called gulfs, make up the natural area: Big Creek, Collins, and Savage. Trails penetrate all three of the gulfs, paralleling the rims with expansive overlooks, descending into the gorges past numerous waterfalls, and providing the solitude and rugged terrain hikers and backpackers seek.

Two entrance stations provide trail access. The Savage Gulf Entrance lies on the east side of the natural area. South of Spencer on TN 111, or north of Dunlap on TN 8/111, turn southwest on TN 399 and at 5.5 miles turn right at the Savage Gulf State Natural Area sign into the parking area and the ranger station at the Savage Gulf Entrance. Or from US 41 in Tracy City, take TN 56 north for 10.3 miles. Turn right on TN 108 and travel through Gruetli–Laager. Turn northeast on TN 399 and from there it's 5.1 miles to the Savage Gulf Entrance.

The Stone Door Entrance lies on the west side of the natural area. Heading north from Tracy City on TN 56, continue straight through the junction with TN 108 in 10.3 miles. Stay straight on TN 56 through Altamont, reaching Beersheba Springs in another 10.4 miles. Or from McMinnville to the north, take TN 56 to the south to climb the side of the plateau to reach Beersheba Springs. In the community, turn east on a side road marked with a sign for the natural area. In 1.1 miles, enter the natural area and reach the Stone Door Entrance in another 0.4 mile.

11 | SAVAGE DAY LOOP

Distance: 4.2-mile loop (Savage Falls Overlook 1.5 miles one way; Rattlesnake Point Overlook 2.0 miles one way)
Difficulty: Easy
Elevation Change: 130 ft
Cautions: High bluffs, stream crossings
Connections: South Rim Trail, North Rim Trail

Attractions: This easy loop with outstanding views offers a quick introduction to the Savage Gulf State Natural Area. Savage Creek sidesteps 30

View of Savage Gulf from Rattlesnake Point

feet down Savage Falls, and Rattlesnake Point Overlook offers a long-distance view down Savage Gulf, named for an early settler, Samuel Savage. Camping is available at the Savage Station Campsites behind the ranger station.

A dedication plaque at Rattlesnake Point tells of Samuel H. Werner Jr. and his wife, Ellen Young Werner, who purchased 3,800 acres in Savage Gulf in 1924–26 and protected and preserved the gulf forest, which became part of the state natural area in 1973. Approximately 500 acres in Savage Gulf along Savage Creek below Savage Falls were never logged, so today the stand of hemlock, yellow poplar, oak, ash, basswood, beech, maple, and hickory is one of the largest old-growth remnants of the mixed mesophytic region of the Eastern deciduous forest. The importance of the forest is recognized in its designation as a National Natural Landmark.

Trailhead: Start at the Savage Gulf Entrance. To the right of the ranger station is a registration stand for day hikers.

Description: Turn left up the trail. Skirt an open field behind the ranger station and pass the Savage Station Campsites on your left at 0.1 mile; there's a water spigot there and restrooms at the ranger station. The trail then meanders through a forest sprinkled with holly and, in late April and early May, pink lady's slipper orchids. In late May, the way is laced with pale pink laurel blossoms.

Cross two streams on boardwalks. At 0.4 mile a laurel canopy shelters the trail as it approaches a suspension bridge across Boyd Branch. At 1.0 mile is the loop junction. Stay straight here to walk the loop clockwise; the return route is to the right. At 1.2 miles at a junction, the South Rim Trail (Hike 12) leads straight ahead. Turn right to continue the loop trail.

At 1.5 miles, a 0.1-mile side trail left takes you to a rock shelf vantage point to view Savage Falls. Savage Creek spills 30 feet over a ledge into a

59

plunge pool, then tumbles past the overlook as it continues its journey through Savage Gulf.

Back on the main trail, continue on until at 2.0 miles Rattlesnake Point Overlook provides a long, deep view of Savage Gulf.

Continue on the loop and at 2.2 miles the North Rim Trail (Hike 13) joins the loop on the left. Stay right here. Cross an old roadbed at 2.4 miles. At 2.8 miles, the trail follows an old narrow-gauge logging railbed that dates from the 1920s; cinders crunch underfoot. At 3.2 miles, return to the loop junction. Turn left, and retrace your steps the 1.0 mile back to the ranger station.

Savage Falls

12 | SOUTH RIM TRAIL

**Distance: 5.8 miles one way (Savage Falls 0.5 mile
   one way)**
Difficulty: Easy
Elevation Change: 100 ft
Cautions: Stream crossings, high bluffs
Connections: Savage Day Loop, Collins Gulf Trail, Stage-
   coach Road Historic Trail

Attractions: This plateautop trail passes above Savage Falls then skirts the south rim of Savage Gulf, offering a number of outstanding gulf views. Along the rim, the trail passes above the old-growth forest in the depths of the gulf. Camping is available at Savage Falls Camp Area and Stage Road Camp Area.

Trailhead: Start at the Savage Gulf Entrance. To the right of the ranger station is a registration stand for day hikers. Turn left up the trail. Pass the Savage Station Campsites on your left at 0.1 mile; there's a water spigot there and restrooms at the ranger station. At 1.0 mile, intersect the Savage Day Loop junction (Hike 11). Stay straight to walk the loop clockwise another 1.2 miles to the junction with the South Rim Trail. Total one-way hike from the trailhead is 7.0 miles.

Description: From the beginning of the South Rim Trail at its junction with the Savage Day Loop, descend to cross Savage Creek on a suspension bridge. The old Werner logging railroad grade runs up the bank straight ahead, but the trail leads right, joins the old Savage Falls road for a few feet, and turns right again passing beneath a canopy of rhododendron along the cascading Savage Creek.

At 0.5 mile is a rock overlook just above Savage Falls where the creek churns and turns over the rock shelf below the overlook. A wooden stairway down to the left leads to the base of the falls. The area downstream is designated a minimal use area to protect the old-growth forest in the depths of the gulf. A permit is required to enter this restricted area.

From the overlook, ascend the hill, passing mammoth boulders, to reach the Savage Falls Camp Area at 0.6 mile. The trail bears right and at 0.7 mile crosses Laurel Branch on a metal footbridge before ascending gently to the plateautop.

You'll reach Curvy Oak Overlook at 1.0 mile, Step Down Overlook at 1.3 miles, and Champion Overlook at 1.6 miles to the right on short side paths. All three allow a look back on Savage Creek and across the gulf to the north rim.

At 1.9 miles, cross Rhododendron Branch on a wooden bridge. The trail then drifts from the bluff's rim to cross occasional small tributaries and at

3.7 miles passes the remains of an old moonshine still on the left. Cross an old roadbed. At 4.0 miles, Laurel Bluff is the first, and best, in a series of overlooks reached by side trails to the right. You'll reach Tulip Tree Overlook at 4.1 miles, Shaky Rock Overlook at 4.3 miles, and Lichen Rock Overlook at 4.5 miles.

The Stage Road Camp Area is at 4.8 miles. A little farther down the trail, a small spring at the bottom of the hill below the campsite is the water source. The trail then crosses the spit of land separating Savage Gulf and Collins Gulf and at 5.5 miles skirts the edge of Collins Gulf.

Ascend, bearing left, to walk across the level top of Peak Mountain. Then drop down a laurel-covered bank to a flat-rock creek crossing and step up to a junction with the old McMinnville–Chattanooga Stagecoach Road at 5.8 miles. A few feet downhill to the right, the Collins Gulf Trail (Hike 15) begins on the left and the Stagecoach Road Historic Trail continues down into the gulf. If you're not headed one of these ways, retrace your walk back along the South Rim to the ranger station parking area.

The junction of the South Rim, Collins Gulf, and Stagecoach Road Trails can be reached along a gravel logging road. At 1.2 miles southwest on TN 399 from the Savage Gulf Entrance, turn right on the gravel road and proceed 1.3 miles to a fork, then continue down the road to the right for another 1.3 miles to enter the natural area; this is an undeveloped access point. You may not be able to drive this old road to the natural area entrance; when the road gets too rough to continue, park beside the road and walk to the entrance. Entering the natural area on foot, walk straight down the road another 0.7 mile to where the road drops to cross a creek and reach a junction with the old Stagecoach Road; to the right a few paces is the trail junction with the South Rim and Collins Gulf Trails.

13 | NORTH RIM AND NORTH PLATEAU TRAILS

Distance: 13.4-mile loop (Hobbs Cabin Camp Area 6.3 miles one way)
Difficulty: Moderate
Elevation Change: 200 ft
Cautions: High bluffs, creek crossings, ticks in summer on North Plateau Trail
Connections: Savage Day Loop, Mountain Oak Trail, Connector Trail

Attractions: The 6.3-mile North Rim Trail and the 7.1-mile North Plateau Trail combine to provide a walk with little elevation change that loops by numerous overlooks of Savage Gulf. The North Rim Trail has more overlooks than any other trail on the South Cumberland. From these view-points, you'll see the confluence of tributary gorges with Savage Gulf, old-growth forest in the bottom of the gorge, the scars of avalanches, and the junction of the three gulfs that make up the state natural area. Hobbs Cabin, at the junction of the North Rim Trail with the North Plateau Trail, may be used for overnight stays, first come, first served; tent camping is also available there and at the Dinky Line Camp Area. The North Plateau Trail passes over Cagle Knobs and toward the end follows the old Dinky Line logging railroad grade; *dinky* referred to the narrow gauge of the rail line.

Trailhead: Start at the Savage Gulf Entrance. To the right of the ranger station, turn left up the Savage Day Loop (Hike 11) and pass the Savage Station Campsites. At 1.0 mile at the Savage Day Loop junction, turn left or right to access the North Rim Trail. To the left, the trail can be reached in another 1.2 miles, passing the South Rim Trail (Hike 12) along the way. To the right the trail can be reached in 1.0 mile.

Description: From the upper end of the Savage Day Loop, the North Rim Trail heads north, crossing Meadow Creek on a suspension bridge at 0.3 mile. Turn left and climb 100 yards to a junction with the North Plateau Trail, which is the return route for this hike; the Dinky Line Camp Area lies 1.4 miles along that trail to the right. Stay straight, following the North Rim Trail, which passes through a dry uplands forest of pine, oak, and mountain laurel.

At 0.6 mile is the Meadow Creek Overlook, where Meadow Creek joins Savage Creek below. At 0.7 mile, a short path left leads out to the Savage Creek Overlook, where the creek washes down the gulf, hidden by trees. Loose Rock Overlook is to the left at 1.4 miles, now getting overgrown.

At 1.7 miles, another short trail left leads to an overlook that provides a view across Savage Gulf to where a rock slide in 1984 took out a strip of forest on the south side of the gulf. Because of the unstable gulf walls, the old-growth forest in the bottom contains trees not as old as might be expected. Compared to old-growth stands in the Great Smoky Mountains, which contain trees as much as 500 years old, the trees in Savage Gulf are younger, perhaps only 400 years old. Periodically, the walls of the gulf collapse, pushing over the trees below. The forest then begins again, as it is doing here, where second growth is reclaiming the slope.

Ford Lick Creek at 2.0 miles; there's a view of Lick Creek Gulf and another view shortly after where this tributary gulf joins Savage Gulf. The trail passes Quartz Pebble Overlook at 2.5 miles, and at 2.6 miles a short path left leads to an overlook of Jumpin' Water Gulf. The trail turns up along this tributary gulf to a junction at 2.8 miles with the Mountain Oak Trail to the right that cuts across the loop to a junction with the North Plateau Trail, forming a shorter loop between the North Rim and North Plateau Trails of 9.6 miles from the trailhead parking area. Beyond the Mountain Oak Trail, ford Jumpin' Water Branch at 2.9 miles.

For the next 3.0 miles, the trail takes you by many overlooks: Jumpin'

Hobbs Cabin

Water at 3.3 miles, Yellow Bluff at 3.5 miles, Over Pine at 3.6 miles (at 4.3 miles cross a small stream with a waterfall to the left), Trail Edge at 4.7 miles, Tommy Point at 5.0 miles, and Split Rock at 6.1 miles. From the two overlooks at Tommy Point, you can see south to the junction of the three gulfs that make up the Savage Gulf State Natural Area: Savage, Collins, and Big Creek. The last part of the trail parallels Coppinger Gulf, a tributary gorge of Savage Gulf; the view from Split Rock is of Coppinger Gulf.

At 6.3 miles is the end of the North Rim Trail and the beginning of the North Plateau Trail straight ahead at a four-way junction. The Connector Trail (Hike 14), which descends left into Coppinger Gulf, takes you across to the other side of the natural area to the Stone Door. The Hobbs Cabin Camp Area is up the hill to the right. You can set up a tent at the campsite, or in the log cabin you can lay out a sleeping bag on a bunk if there is still an empty one. The cabin is a newer construction replacing an old hunting cabin. Behind the cabin, down the hill, a spring provides water.

Walking the North Plateau Trail straight ahead, continue along Coppinger Gulf, swinging right and then back to the edge at an overlook at 6.4 miles; to the left you can see the main canyon of Savage Gulf. The trail turns northeast away from Coppinger Gulf to descend to a crossing of Stairway Creek at 6.8 miles.

The trail then makes a long traverse through plateau forest, occasionally dropping into swales and marsh areas, some wet enough to support stands of cinnamon and New York ferns. At 7.0 miles, the trail crosses an old road that led to the old Hobbs Cabin. Cross another old road at 8.1 miles that is gated 50 yards to the left. Soon after, cross another roadbed. At 8.6 miles, the trail passes a small open area where exposed rock covered in reindeer moss has prevented trees from growing. Cross another road at 9.0 miles.

The trail crosses a small stream, probably dry in summer, and turns upstream for a time where the stream channel is thick with mountain laurel.

As the trail turns south, it approaches Meadow Creek at 10.1 miles on your left, also covered in laurel. The trail passes through an older second-growth forest of oak and hickory with occasional shortleaf pines.

Ascend into low hills called Cagle Knobs and wander through the hills to cross another old road at the top of the knobs at 11.4 miles. The trail then descends, crossing another old road, to a junction with the other end of the Mountain Oak Trail at 11.9 miles; the North Rim Trail lies 0.8 mile to the right. Stay straight to the Dinky Line Camp Area at 12.0 miles. After the side path into the campsite, the main trail crosses two wet-weather streams that are the source of water for the campsite; in dry times of the year, you must bring water with you. Beyond the stream crossings, the trail joins the old Dinky Line railbed; the path is covered in cinders.

Near the end of the loop is what appears to be a junction with a horizontal double blaze on a tree. This indicates a road nearby for rescuers; do not turn left here. Stay straight to a junction at 13.4 miles with the North Rim Trail, closing the loop. Turn left to head back to the Savage Day Loop in 0.3 mile, and then back to the ranger station either way on the loop. Total hiking distance round-trip from the ranger station is 17.9 miles.

14 | CONNECTOR TRAIL

Distance: 6.7 miles one way
Difficulty: Strenuous
Elevation Change: 800 ft
Cautions: Creek crossings, boulder fields
Connections: North Rim Trail, North Plateau Trail, Stage-
coach Road Historic Trail, Collins Gulf Trail, Big Creek
Gulf Trail

Attractions: The Connector Trail connects the major trails in the Savage Gulf State Natural Area and is the only trail giving access from one side of the natural area to the other, crossing the three main gulfs along the way. At rare times of high water, the Connector Trail is impassable. A side trail leads to the Decatur Savage Historic Site. The original cabin, built in 1910, had some later additions, but they were removed when the cabin site was included in the natural area. Cator Savage, who built the original cabin, was a descendant of Samuel Savage, the early settler for whom Savage Gulf is named. Camping is available at Hobbs Cabin and the Sawmill Camp Area.

Trailhead: Start at the Savage Gulf Entrance. To the right of the ranger station, turn left up the Savage Day Loop (Hike 11) and pass the Savage Station Campsites. At 1.0 mile at the Savage Day Loop junction, turn left (1.2 miles) or right (1.0 mile) to access the North Rim Trail. Then walk the North Rim Trail another 6.3 miles to a four-way junction with the North

Plateau Trail (Hike 13) straight ahead, the Hobbs Cabin Camp Area to the right, and the Connector Trail to the left.

Description: From the junction of the North Rim and North Plateau Trails at the Hobbs Cabin Camp Area, turn left on the Connector Trail and descend a very rocky slope into Coppinger Gulf that leads into Savage Gulf. At 1.9 miles the trail reaches Savage Creek, which is dry at the crossing most of the time because the creek flows into a sink upstream from the trail.

After crossing the creekbed, the trail ascends a ridge separating Savage Gulf from Collins Gulf, and then it descends into Collins Gulf. At 3.1 miles, cross the old McMinnville/Chattanooga Stagecoach Road. The Stagecoach Road Historic Trail (Hike 15) turns left here, following the old stage road

Suter Falls

toward the top of the plateau. Continue straight on the Connector Trail to the Collins Gulf Trail junction at 3.5 miles. The Collins Gulf Trail (Hike 15) leads to the left and the Sawmill Camp Area lies to the right. Go straight on the Connector Trail to the crossing of the Collins River at 3.6 miles. Most times of the year the river is dry at the crossing. From the riverbed, ascend over the ridge separating Collins Gulf from Big Creek Gulf.

At 4.2 miles a side trail to the right leads down to the Decatur Savage Historic Site. At 4.8 miles, drop to the Big Creek crossing, which is also dry at the ford most times of the year. Ascend the other side of Big Creek Gulf. The passage down to and up the other side from the creekbed has rough footing because of the rocks and boulders you must walk across. At 6.1 miles, cross Laurel Creek, stepping across large boulders as the creek cascades beneath you down to Big Creek.

The trail then ends at a junction with the Big Creek Gulf Trail (Hike 17) at 6.7 miles. Turn right to ascend the wall of the gulf and emerge through the Great Stone Door. It's then 0.9 mile to the Stone Door Entrance and the ranger station.

15 | COLLINS GULF AND STAGECOACH ROAD HISTORIC TRAILS

Distance: 11.9-mile loop (Suter Falls 0.7 mile one way from Gruetli–Laager access)
Difficulty: Strenuous
Elevation Change: 800 ft
Cautions: Stream and river crossings, high bluffs, rocky footing
Connections: South Rim Trail, Connector Trail

Attractions: The 9.9-mile Collins Gulf Trail and the 1.6-mile Stagecoach Road Historic Trail combine with a short piece of the Connector Trail to make one of the most fascinating loop hikes on the South Cumberland, with numerous overlooks and waterfalls, including Suter Falls. This spreading waterfall, the cascading creek, and the massive rock walls of the gorge around Suter Falls make this setting one of the true spectacles of the Southeast. Camping is available at the Collins West Camp Area, Sawmill Camp Area, and Collins East Camp Area.

The Stagecoach Road Historic Trail follows the old route of the Stagecoach Road that ran from McMinnville to Chattanooga. Construction of the road began in 1830 and depended heavily on slave labor. The old roadbed, with its rock walls and stone cribbing, is on the National Register of Historic Places.

Trailhead: The remote Collins Gulf and Stagecoach Road Historic Trails

Horsepound Falls

can be accessed along the South Rim Trail (Hike 12) and the Connector Trail (Hike 14) out of the Savage Gulf Entrance. But a newly developed entry near the community of Gruetli–Laager provides more direct access. Head southwest on TN 399 from the Savage Gulf Entrance 5.1 miles to the junction of TN 108 in Gruetli–Laager; turn right and in 2.0 miles turn right again on 55th Avenue. Or if you are on the other side of the natural area at the Great Stone Door entrance, head south on TN 50 through Altamont to a junction with TN 108, where you turn left for 3.0 miles to a left turn on 55th Avenue. After the turn onto 55th, drive 2.7 miles to a parking area on the left where the main road makes a sharp right turn. From the parking area, walk down an old road 0.2 mile to its end; pass a spring on the left and then take a path left that crosses a bridge over a stream. The path continues through the woods to a junction at 0.3 mile with a trail right to the Collins West Camp Area and to the bluff for the impressive view at Collins Gulf Overlook. Campers might find water in the spring along the trail into the camp area; otherwise, water is available from Rocky Mountain Creek down the main trail. At the junction, stay to the left to reach the edge of the bluff at 0.4 mile and another side path to the right that leads to the Collins West Camp Area. From here you must make a short, steep descent, bearing right, down the bluff to connect with the Collins Gulf Trail at 0.6 mile.

Description: At the junction with the Collins Gulf Trail, turn left to hike the loop clockwise; the path straight will be the return route. Skirt a rock wall on the left and Rocky Mountain Creek on the right, which flows through a cascade and then a 20-foot waterfall. Water often drips from the rock wall, so the trail gets iced over in winter. A line strung on posts serves as a guardrail; proceed with caution.

The trail then passes under a huge overhang along a curved rock wall and at 0.1 mile fords the creek just below Suter Falls, an impressive 40-foot waterfall named for a nearby landowner in Gruetli.

The creek crossing below Suter Falls can be difficult at high water; take care. After crossing, turn up left to follow the bluff, crossing a small stream at 0.4 mile with a waterfall up to the left. Pass between the bluff and a huge pile of rocks and then a large chestnut oak to the right at 0.6 mile; the trail begins a descent into Collins Gulf. After several switchbacks down to the Collins River, the trail joins an old road that parallels the river downstream. At 1.9 miles, a path leads to the right to Horsepound Falls, a broad waterfall in the river. At 2.2 miles, cross a branch of Fall Creek if the water is up; just to the left the main stem of the creek disappears into a sinkhole.

At 3.2 miles, the trail crosses the Collins River, dry here most times of the year because the water upstream has sunk below the rocks of the riverbed. At times of high water, the river ford is impassable. Once on the other side, continue downstream, passing a side trail at 3.5 miles that leads back across the riverbed and up the trace of an old road to a spring where campers get water. At 3.7 miles the Collins Gulf Trail ends at the junction with the Connector Trail; straight ahead lies the Sawmill Camp Area. Turn right on the Connector Trail until at 4.1 miles you reach a junction with the old Stagecoach Road. Turn right up the road to begin the Stagecoach Road Historic Trail.

Following the washed-out route of the old road, the trail ascends the slope of Collins Gulf; the footing is sometimes rough. At 5.2 miles, pass a tall wet-weather waterfall up to the left. At 5.5 miles, rock terracing holds up the hillside and rock walls keep the old roadbed in place. At 5.6 miles, cross the stream from another wet-weather waterfall and the road makes a hairpin turn up left. Notice the rock cribbing that holds the road in place. There's a junction with the Collins Gulf Trail to the right at 5.7 miles and a little farther the South Rim Trail (Hike 12) to the left.

Turn right on the Collins Gulf Trail, which heads up the slope. Reach the plateautop and swing out to the rim of Collins Gulf. A side trail right at 6.2 miles leads to Blue Branch Overlook, with a great view of the junction of the Blue Branch Gulf with Collins Gulf.

The trail heads up the tributary gulf to descend into a laurel and rhododendron thicket to a boulder crossing of Blue Branch at 6.8 miles. The trail then heads back out to the rim of Collins Gulf, where at 7.5 miles a short side path to the right leads to Horsepound Point Overlook. Across the way is the tributary gulf of Fall Creek. At 8.1 miles, a path right leads to Standing Stone Overlook.

At 8.2 miles the trail crosses exposed rock that seems to offer a view, but there is none, so stay on the trail to avoid trampling the reindeer moss (actually a lichen). Drop from the rock to cross a small stream that forms a small waterfall to your right, where it cascades into the gulf. At 8.4 miles watch for a path right to the Collins River Overlook.

At 8.8 miles, the trail drops to cross two branches of a stream; at the second you'll see the remains of a moonshine still to the left. Crossing a stream at 10.4 miles, you'll see the remains of some barrels that probably mark the spot of another still.

At 10.6 miles is the Collins East Camp Area to the left, where the trail makes a right turn. Water is available at the last creek crossing, which may be dry in summer, or from the river farther down the trail. After the campsite, the trail crosses an old road and then begins a descent, at first gradual and then more steeply and down a rock shelf, to a crossing of the Collins River on a suspension bridge at 11.0 miles. You'll see a jumble of house-size boulders in the riverbed.

The trail now crosses a rocky slope, where you often must boulderhop. At 11.4 miles, emerge from crossing the rocks to connect with the end of an old road, which you then follow below the bluff to the junction to close the loop at 11.9 miles. Continuing straight takes you up to the Collins West Camp Area and out to the trailhead parking in another 0.6 mile.

16 | STONE DOOR TRAIL

Distance: 1.0 mile one way
Difficulty: Easy
Elevation Change: Level
Cautions: High bluffs
Connections: Big Creek Gulf Trail, Big Creek Rim Trail

Attractions: This easy trail affords one of the best views of the gulf area and ends at the Great Stone Door, an impressive crack in the rock bluff

Great Stone Door

Overlook of Laurel Creek Gulf

with a sloping floor that probably was used by Native Americans as a way in and out of Big Creek Gulf. Camping is available at the Stone Door Camp Area near the ranger station.

Trailhead: Start at the Stone Door Entrance. Begin beside the ranger station at the day hiker signup stand. The trail leads to the right and is universally accessible for the first 0.2 mile.

Description: On the paved walk, cross a creekbed on a bridge. A side trail here leads right 0.2 mile up to the Stone Door Camp Area, which can also be reached from the far end of the parking area; there's a water spigot and a privy.

On the main trail, at 0.2 mile, is an overlook of Laurel Creek Gulf, which contains Laurel Creek. The trail, now a dirt path, crosses three bridges. Near the end an old road that's blocked comes in from the right. The trail reaches an intersection at 0.9 mile with the Big Creek Rim Trail (Hike 17) to the right. Left, you can walk down to an overlook of Big Creek Gulf. Straight ahead from the intersection, pass a junction with the Big Creek Gulf Trail, which heads down stone steps to pass through the Great Stone

Door. Past the Stone Door and over a bridge, bear right to make your way out to a grand overlook of Big Creek Gulf below and to the left distant views of the convergence of Collins and Savage Gulfs.

17 BIG CREEK GULF AND BIG CREEK RIM TRAILS

Distance: 7.2-mile loop (Ranger Creek Falls 2.4 miles one way)
Difficulty: Moderate
Elevation Change: 700 ft
Cautions: Rocky footing, small stream crossings, steep ascent
Connections: Stone Door Trail, Connector Trail, Greeter Trail, Laurel Trail

Attractions: The 4.0-mile Big Creek Gulf Trail and the 3.2-mile Big Creek Rim Trail form a loop that penetrates the remote country of this third gorge in the state natural area. Descending through the Great Stone Door to emerge in Big Creek Gulf, the route drops to Big Creek and follows it upstream, passing a side path to Ranger Creek Falls and reaching the sinks of Big Creek, where the stream usually drains below the rocky creekbed to run underground. Ascending from the gulf, the route passes Alum Gap Camp Area and returns along the rim of the gorge, with several overlooks of the deep gulf.

Trailhead: From the Stone Door Entrance, walk the Stone Door Trail (Hike 16) for 0.9 mile to a junction with the Big Creek Rim Trail to the right, which will be the return route. Continue straight a few paces to a junction with the Big Creek Gulf Trail.

Description: Take the Big Creek Gulf Trail down stone steps that descend through the Great Stone Door. The huge crack in the rock allows you to descend below the sandstone rim of the gorge and emerge inside Big Creek Gulf. The trail then descends steeply down the rocky slope; keep an eye on the white blazes. Descend to a junction with the Connector Trail (Hike 14) to the left at 0.9 mile. Turn right up Big Creek Gulf.

The trail parallels Big Creek upstream, crossing rocks much of the time. At 1.2 miles, descend to cross an old logging road; to the left you can walk down to the creek and look across to where springs emerge during the wet seasons.

The main trail follows an old road as it continues upstream along Big Creek. At 1.4 miles, turn right off the road to ascend above the creek and then descend to rejoin the road. Turn right and descend almost to creek level before the trail again turns right off the road, at 1.9 miles. At 2.0 miles

Ranger Creek Falls

the trail rejoins the road at a junction with a 0.4-mile side trail left that leads to Ranger Creek Falls. This blue-blazed trail leads down to Big Creek, right along a channel of the streambed, and then left to cross the creekbed, usually dry at this location; do not attempt the crossing at rare times of high water. On the other side, follow the trail up an old road and then bear left to cross Ranger Creek, also normally dry. Join another old road and follow it up to Ranger Creek Falls, spilling over a 20-foot ledge and disappearing into a sink; such vanishing falls are called terminal waterfalls.

Back on the main trail, ascend steeply on the old road, then turn left at 2.1 miles to descend back to creek level and an unmarked side path at 2.6 miles that leads left to the sinks of Big Creek. Here the creek normally flows into a deep green pool and disappears so that downstream from this spot the creekbed is usually dry, until it reemerges near the springs you saw earlier. In wet weather there's a waterfall to the left of the sinks.

Back on the main trail, watch for a left turn, and then you'll be back on

The sinks of Big Creek

an old road above the creek. The trail connects with another old road and then gets rocky as it ascends. The road eventually begins to descend; cross a cascading stream at 3.1 miles. Later, the trail narrows and climbs the slope with switchbacks and stone steps to emerge on an old logging road at 3.8 miles. Turn left and follow the old road up to Alum Gap at the plateau rim; Alum Gap Branch cascades down on your left.

Into the gap, the Big Creek Gulf Trail ends at 4.0 miles at a junction with the Greeter Trail (Hike 20) and Laurel Trail (Hike 19) to the left. Turn right on the Big Creek Rim Trail to pass through the Alum Gap Camp Area. Water is available from Alum Gap Branch, which can also be reached 0.1 mile down the Greeter Trail; in summer the branch may be dry, so bring water up from the gulf.

The trail follows the rim of Big Creek Gulf. At 4.5 miles is Big Creek Overlook, where a distant view to the right reveals the depths of the gulf. Arrive at Pine Rock Overlook at 4.7 miles. And then at 5.6 miles the trail passes the Sinks Overlook; across the gulf you can see a low rock wall at the location where Big Creek sinks into the streambed.

The trail then reaches Split Rock Overlook at 6.9 miles, where you'll see the rock walls around the Stone Door to the far left. Soon after, the trail joins an old road. There's a side trail right that leads down to the bluff edge, but there's no view. At 7.2 miles the loop ends atop the Great Stone Door at the junction of the Stone Door and Big Creek Gulf Trails. It's 0.9 mile on the Stone Door Trail back to the ranger station.

18 | LAUREL FALLS LOOP

Distance: 0.3-mile loop
Difficulty: Moderate
Elevation Change: 75 ft
Cautions: Steep rocky descent
Connections: Laurel Trail, Stone Door Trail

Attractions: This short loop descends to an overlook of Laurel Falls, where Laurel Creek drops 25 feet into a pool below a lip of rock with a hollowed-out amphitheater behind. At the site of the Laurel Mill, you'll see foundation stones from a mill that once operated creekside using water for power, at separate times perhaps grinding grain and cutting lumber.

Trailhead: At the Stone Door Entrance, the Laurel Falls Loop begins on the right side of the ranger station near the beginning of the Stone Door Trail (Hike 16). The Laurel Trail (Hike 19) begins to the left of the ranger station.

Description: On the right side of the ranger station is the loop junction of the Laurel Falls Loop, straight and right. Turn down the trail to the right

Laurel Falls in Savage Gulf State National Area

to hike counterclockwise; the trail straight ahead will be the return route. The gravel path drops to a steep, rocky descent that leads down the side of the small gorge of Laurel Creek; step carefully. At the bottom at 0.1 mile, walk onto a wooden platform that offers a view of Laurel Falls.

From the overlook, continue to the left and down steps to the expanse of rock at the top of the falls; take care near the edge. Turn left along the edge of rock and back into the woods to a junction with the main trail left. Keep straight to walk past a rocky drainage beside the road and down to the creek at 0.2 mile to the site of Laurel Mill.

Back at the junction, head up steps to a left turn near the road and ascend the slope back to the ranger station to complete the loop at 0.3 mile.

19 | LAUREL TRAIL

Distance: 2.9 miles one way
Difficulty: Easy
Elevation Change: 50 ft
Cautions: None
Connections: Laurel Falls Loop, Stone Door Trail, Big Creek Rim Trail, Big Creek Gulf Trail, Greeter Trail

Attractions: This trail can be used to form loop hikes. The Laurel Trail forms a 7.0-mile loop with the Stone Door and Big Creek Rim Trails and a 7.8-mile loop with the Stone Door and Big Creek Gulf Trails. Camping is available at the Stone Door Camp Area (near the ranger station) and at the Alum Gap Camp Area, at the intersection with the Big Creek Gulf and Big Creek Rim Trails.

Trailhead: At the Stone Door Entrance, the Laurel Trail begins to the left of the ranger station near the beginning of the Stone Door Trail (Hike 16) and the Laurel Falls Loop (Hike 18).

Description: Heading west on the Laurel Trail, cross the entrance road at 0.1 mile, pass under a powerline, and soon cross a bridge over a drainage area. The trail then leads through second-growth forest, dipping through several hollows and low areas, some of which can be muddy or have streams in wet weather. At 1.4 miles, if the leaves are off the trees in winter, you'll see a pond to the right outside the natural area. Watch for a huge patch of club moss at 2.1 miles to the right of the trail. At 2.7 miles, you'll see small piles of rocks on the left at an old homesite.

The trail ends at 2.9 miles at the intersection at Alum Gap, with the Big Creek Rim Trail (Hike 17) straight ahead and the Big Creek Gulf Trail (Hike 17) and Greeter Trail (Hike 20) to the right. The Alum Gap Camp Area is just down the Big Creek Rim Trail. .

20 GREETER FALLS LOOP/GREETER TRAIL

Distance: 1.8 miles one way (Greeter Falls 0.5 mile one way; Blue Hole 0.6 mile one way; Greeter Falls Loop 1.1 miles)
Difficulty: Moderate
Elevation Change: 250 ft
Cautions: Stream crossings, rough footing, steep descents
Connections: Big Creek Gulf Trail, Big Creek Rim Trail, Laurel Trail

Attractions: This trail combination features Upper and Lower Greeter Falls and Boardtree Falls and a walk to one of the best views in the natural area. Greeter Falls was named for the Greeter Family, who sold the land to the state to add to the state natural area. The amphitheater of Greeter Falls is

Greeter Falls

unusual, with a thick sandstone layer on top of a more crumbly limestone layer. Most waterfalls on the plateau spill over hard sandstone that caps layers of softer sandstone or shale. A side trail leads to Blue Hole, a great swimming hole on a hot day. Camping is available at the Alum Gap Camp Area, at the intersection with Big Creek Gulf and Big Creek Rim Trails.

Trailhead: On TN 56, 4.3 miles south of the Stone Door turnoff in Beersheba Springs, turn east onto the second road for the Greeter Pines subdivision development. At 0.7 mile, there's a parking area on the left. (In 1992, the Savage Gulf Preservation League purchased this lot to protect access to Greeter Falls.) The trail begins at the gated road across from the parking area.

Description: Walk the road into the woods, following the white trail blazes. At 0.1 mile at a junction is a registration stand for day hikers. A side trail leads right 0.5 mile to the Blue Hole, a pool 10 to 20 feet deep on Firescald Creek. The area above Blue Hole is where Longs Mill once stood, at the junction of Piney and Firescald Creeks. The park has long-range plans for additional trails in the area.

Stay with the main trail left at the junction with the Blue Hole Trail to head toward Greeter Falls. At 0.2 mile a trail up to the left leads 50 yards to the old Greeter Homeplace, dating from the 1800s; there are still foundations and a water well. The trail curves right at this junction and joins another old roadway; back to the left the road is overgrown. At 0.3 mile, the trail turns right off the road you're walking. Straight ahead will be the return part of the Greeter Falls Loop.

The trail follows a small stream, dry in summer, down to where the forest opens up at the edge of the small gulf of Firescald Creek. Curve left along the edge of the bluff past a fragmented wall colored with iron deposits and lichen. Pass under a large rock overhang and descend steeply to a side trail on the right at 0.4 mile that leads to the Upper and Lower Greeter Falls. As you step down from the main trail, there's a junction with the upper falls to the right and the lower falls to the left. Walk 100 yards to the right to descend to the upper falls, a straight rock ledge 15 feet high and 30 feet long, where Firescald Creek spills onto a large sandstone boulder. The creek then floats 100 feet to slip over the top of the Lower Greeter Falls.

To get to a view of the lower falls, return to the junction and take the left trail. This 0.1-mile trail to the falls leads to a spiral metal staircase that descends the rock bluff to the slope. At the bottom of the stairs, turn right. (The trail to the left was an old route to the falls that is now abandoned.) To the right is a long wooden stairway that leads down to the edge of the plunge pool, where Greeter Falls splashes from a height of 50 feet. Step off the stairway onto a board across a slanted rock; even with crosspieces to aid with footing, the board can be slippery when wet, so take care.

Back on the main trail, continue by ascending along the base of the bluff. At 0.5 mile, a path to the right is the old access that is now abandoned; stay left. Pass under a large overhang, descend across a boulder field, and then begin another ascent. Boardtree Creek to your right creates Boardtree Falls: a double drop, a slide down a sloped wall, and then ribbons of water splashing into a rock pile 10 feet below.

Before reaching the creek above the falls, you'll find a side trail to the left at 0.7 mile that is the return loop. If you're just out to see the waterfalls and want to return to the parking area, turn left here. Just up this trail, rejoin the old roadway and turn left to return to the loop junction at 0.8 mile, then continue straight and bear right to return to the parking lot in another 0.3 mile.

At the junction beside Boardtree Falls, the Greeter Trail continues straight. Cross the creek on a suspension bridge just above the falls and climb through a laurel thicket to the plateautop for a level walk with Greeter Gulf to your right. At 1.6 miles, the trail meets the end of an old road; take the short side trail right to Big Bluffs Overlook, which provides an open view down Big Creek Gulf.

Continue on the main trail along the old road. Bear right off the road and drop to a crossing of the intermittent Alum Gap Branch at 1.7 miles. As you ascend from the creek, the trail turns left and reaches a junction at 1.8 miles at Alum Gap with the Laurel Trail (Hike 19) left, the Big Creek Gulf Trail (Hike 17) right, and the Big Creek Rim Trail (Hike 17) straight ahead through the Alum Gap Camp Area.

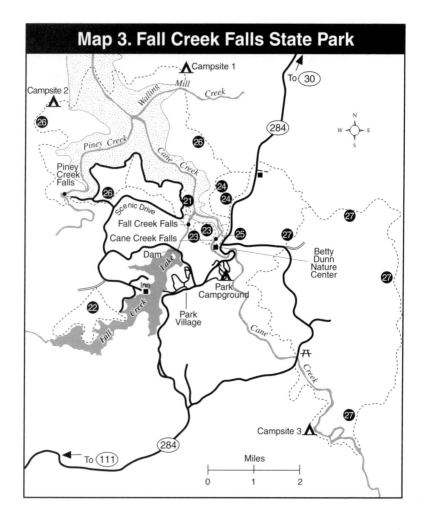

Map 3. Fall Creek Falls State Park

Campsite 1

To 30

Campsite 2

Walling   Mill   Creek

26

Piney   Creek

Cane   Creek

284

N
W   E
S

26

Piney
Creek
Falls

26

Scenic Drive

21

24

24

Fall Creek Falls

27

Cane Creek Falls

23

23

25

27

Dam

Lake

Betty
Dunn
Nature
Center

27

Inn

Park
Campground

22

Fall   Creek

Park
Village

Cane   Creek

27

Campsite 3

To 111

284

Miles

0   1   2

FALL CREEK FALLS STATE PARK

With enough facilities to be rated a resort park and enough remaining wilderness to satisfy hikers and backpackers, Fall Creek Falls State Park is Tennessee's premier state park. Here visitors can stay in a lodge and cabins or camp in the large campground, play tennis and golf or lounge by the pool, and go bike-riding, fishing, or boating on the lake. Meanwhile, the unaltered gorges below the rim wait for hikers to come and enjoy the uninterrupted solitude and silence. Trails lead into Cane Creek Gorge and past numerous waterfalls. These are the main attractions: waterfalls of varied height and width with several stages between cascade and true fall of water, including Fall Creek Falls, the tallest waterfall in the eastern United States.

Fall Creek Falls State Park lies to the north of Savage Gulf State Natural Area. On TN 111 between Spencer to the north and Dunlap to the south, turn east on TN 284 to enter the park at the south entrance. Or, on TN 30 between Spencer to the north and Pikeville to the southeast, turn on TN 284 to enter the park at the north entrance. TN 284 travels through the park, giving access to the nature center, where you can get information, and the park village, with all the accommodations and amenities.

21 | FALL CREEK FALLS TRAIL

Distance: 0.4 mile one way
Difficulty: Strenuous
Elevation Loss: 260 ft
Cautions: Steep descent, rough footing, slippery rocks
Connections: Woodland Trail

Attractions: On this trail you'll wind down into Fall Creek Gorge and stand at the base of the 256-foot-high Fall Creek Falls, the tallest waterfall in the eastern United States.

Trailhead: Entering the park on TN 284, turn northwest at the park village to cross Fall Creek Lake Dam and turn right at the sign to Fall Creek Falls Scenic Drive. At 0.6 mile from the turn, bear right on the scenic loop drive. At 1.7 miles, turn right into the Fall Creek Falls parking area.

Description: From the parking area take the sidewalk to the Fall Creek Falls overlook at 0.1 mile, where you'll have a bird's-eye view of the tall waterfall. In wet seasons, a smaller waterfall to the right is formed by Coon Creek as it spills into the gorge.

Fall Creek Falls

Right of the overlook, you can walk the Woodland Trail (Hike 23) that leads above the falls. To hike to the bottom of Fall Creek Falls, turn left from the upper overlook, following an orange blaze. Descend a steep rocky path, turn right at some benches to pass below a tall rock wall and overhang, and come face-to-face with the waterfall at 0.4 mile. If the volume of the falls is high, the rocks around the falls are slippery from the mist kicked up by the water as it pounds into rocks at the bottom. While enjoying the mist from the waterfall on your face, prepare for a slow-paced climb back to the parking area.

22 | GILBERT GAUL LOOP

Distance: 4.5 miles
Difficulty: Moderate
Elevation Change: 100 ft
Cautions: Overgrown in places, ticks in summer
Connections: None

Attractions: This loop swings by the site of the Gilbert Gaul Homestead. A painter, Gaul came to the Fall Creek Falls area of Tennessee while in his twenties, inheriting land from an uncle. At the homestead, he built a studio where he completed several of his paintings, including *The Picket*, showing a mountain man standing guard; Gaul used a local moonshiner as the model for the soldier. On the return part of the loop, the trail parallels the shore of Fall Creek Lake, with several waterside views.

Trailhead: From the park village, take Village Road west across Fall Creek Lake Dam. Pass the Fall Creek Falls Scenic Drive to the right and continue, curving south, toward the inn. Just before reaching the inn, which stands at the end of the road, turn right into the fishing cabin area at the lake's edge. At the end of the road in 0.5 mile, next to the last cabin on the left, is the trailhead for the Gilbert Gaul Trail.

Description: From the end of the road, take the footpath straight ahead as it bears right where lake waters reach into a cove. At 0.1 mile, intersect the loop part of the trail; the path straight ahead will be the return route. Turn right to hike the loop counterclockwise.

The trail ascends from this junction to curve left and reach a junction with an old road at 0.2 mile. Turn right on the road and follow it up to a junction with another old road; stay right. At 0.6 mile the road curves left as another road comes in from the right.

The trail reaches a junction with a gravel road at 0.7 mile. To the right the road leads up to a paved road that gives access to a group camp. Turn left to continue the loop hike. The gravel gives way to a dirt road, sometimes sandy, as the trail descends toward the lake.

At 1.6 miles, emerge into an open area and follow the road track across the field to reenter the woods. At the bottom of the field, off to the right, lies the site of the old Gaul Homestead. The park intends to erect a sign to mark the spot.

Walk down to the edge of the lake at 1.9 miles. This is virtually the head of the lake; to the right Fall Creek drains into the lake waters, although from this spot the creek is not readily visible. Turn left to complete the loop back to the trailhead.

The trail follows the shore of Fall Creek Lake, winding through the woods along the shore and dipping through low, wet areas growing moss and New York ferns. At 3.0 miles, walk up to the Frazier Rain Shelter at the edge of the lake.

Continue along the shore of the lake, passing a mound of sticks at the water's edge that is a muskrat den. At 3.8 miles, cross the end of an old road at the lake's edge, the same road the trail followed on the first leg of the hike.

At 4.2 miles, curve left up a cove of the lake, with the cabins across the water to the right. The trail swings around the end of this cove to close the loop at 4.4 miles. Straight ahead, it's another 0.1 mile back to the trailhead.

23 | GORGE OVERLOOK AND WOODLAND TRAILS

Distance: 2.0-mile loop
Difficulty: Moderate
Elevation Change: 200 ft
Cautions: Swinging bridge, steep stairs, high cliffs
Connections: Fall Creek Falls Trail, Lower Cane Creek
Overnight Loop

Attractions: The 0.8-mile Woodland Trail and the 0.7-mile Gorge Overlook Trail combine to make a 2-mile round-trip hike from the Nature Center. The route takes you over Cane Creek Cascade on a suspension bridge, around a blufftop above Cane Creek Gorge with grand views, and then to the top of Fall Creek Falls.

Trailhead: Start at the Betty Dunn Nature Center, located 1.4 miles into the park from the north entrance. At an intersection, turn right into parking for the nature center, named for a former governor's wife who took an interest in the park and encouraged development of the facilities.

Description: Behind the nature center, a sidewalk leading right takes you down to a platform where you'll look up at 45-foot-high Cane Creek Cascade. Just downstream to the right is the top of Cane Creek Falls, which can be seen from an overlook on the north side of the nature center.

To walk the Woodland Trail, marked with a yellow blaze, bear left behind the nature center to a suspension bridge that stretches across Cane Creek above the cascade. Cross the bridge and turn right, switching back and climbing steep wooden steps before turning right again. The trail straight at the top of the steps leads to the park campground.

At 0.2 mile, turn right on the Gorge Overlook Trail, marked with a red blaze; the Woodland Trail straight ahead will be the return route. (There's also an occasional white blaze because this is part of the Lower Cane Creek Overnight Trail.) Descend through a forest of mixed hardwood. At 0.4 mile a spur trail to the right leads to an overlook of Cane Creek Falls. As you

Cane Creek Cascade

approach the overlook, you'll see Rockhouse Falls, a slender 125-foot stream of water sharing the same plunge basin with the more robust 85-foot Cane Creek Falls on the right. This is one of the trail's best views.

Back on the main trail, continue the loop, which drops gently through a shaded hemlock passageway into a forest of tall mixed hardwoods. At 0.6 mile a spur trail right offers a view of Cane Creek Gorge, the main drainage of the park's watershed; you can also see the joining of the Fall Creek Gorge to the left. Back on the main trail, you'll soon approach side trails to Rocky Point Overlook and then to the Fall Creek Gorge Overlook.

At 0.9 mile, the Gorge Overlook Trail rejoins the Woodland Trail. Before turning left to complete the loop back to the nature center, turn right on the Woodland Trail toward the Fall Creek Falls Overlook. The trail crosses a wooden bridge over Fall Creek, red and pungent from sulfur and iron oxides released from rock exposed in 1968 during the excavation for the Fall Creek Lake Dam upstream. Then through a canopy of rhododendron, an unofficial side trail right leads to the rock ledge where Fall Creek slips over the edge into the gorge below; use caution. Continue on the main trail, crossing Coon Creek on a wooden bridge, pass the junction with the Lower

Cane Creek Overnight Loop (Hike 26) on the left, and arrive at the Fall Creek Falls Overlook and the junction with the Fall Creek Falls Trail (Hike 21) at 1.2 miles.

Retrace your steps to the junction of the Gorge Overlook Trail and continue down the Woodland Trail to the junction with the beginning of the Gorge Overlook Trail at 1.8 miles and then back to the nature center.

24 | PAW PAW TRAIL

Distance: 5.0-mile loop
Difficulty: Easy
Elevation Change: 200 ft
Cautions: Rough footing, stream crossings
Connections: Cable Trail, Lower Cane Creek
   Overnight Loop

Attractions: This loop combines views with a walk through woods of laurel, rhododendron, hemlock, and mixed hardwoods.

Trailhead: Start at the Betty Dunn Nature Center, located 1.4 miles into the park from the north entrance on the main road through the park. The loop begins north of the parking area in front of the nature center.

Description: Follow the blazes down through a stand of rhododendron. The trail is blazed with orange markings, but there are also white blazes because this is part of the Lower Cane Creek Overnight Loop (Hike 26). At 0.2 mile the trail comes up to the road at a crossing of Rockhouse Creek; cross on the road bridge if the water is up. The trail then passes the Cable Trail (Hike 25) on the left. Stay straight to remain on the Paw Paw Loop.

The trail climbs a short distance, then levels for a pleasant stroll. At 0.4 mile a spur trail leads left to the Cane Creek Falls Overlook, where you'll have a view of the waterfall.

At 0.5 mile, the main trail reaches the loop junction; the path right is the return of the Paw Paw Trail and also the route of the Lower Cane Creek Overnight Loop (Hike 26). Turn left, and at 1.0 mile a spur trail left leads to an overlook of Cane Creek Gorge. Continue on the main trail, crossing Paw Paw Creek, named for the local pawpaw tree, which has purple flowers and an edible fruit. At 1.5 miles a side trail leads to an overlook that offers a distant view of Fall Creek Falls.

At 2.5 miles is a junction with the Lower Cane Creek Overnight Loop to the left; the loop also continues straight on the Paw Paw Trail. Cross Paw Paw Creek on a footbridge and at 2.6 miles reach a junction with the overnight trail turning off to the left. Turn right at this junction to complete the Paw Paw Loop. The trail passes through woods paralleling the north entrance road. At 4.5 miles, close the loop; it's then a half mile back to the parking area.

25 | CABLE TRAIL

Distance: 0.2 mile one way
Difficulty: Strenuous
Elevation Loss: 120 ft
Cautions: Rugged, steep drop, difficult footing
Connections: Paw Paw Loop, Lower Cane Creek
   Overnight Loop

Attractions: You can hang onto a cable as you progress down a 100-foot rugged rock chute to stand across the creek from the base of Rockhouse and Cane Creek Falls.

Trailhead: Start at the Betty Dunn Nature Center, 1.4 miles into the park from the north entrance on the main road through the park. Take the Paw Paw Loop (Hike 24)—also part of the Lower Cane Creek Overnight Loop (Hike 26)—which begins north of the parking area in front of the nature center. Crossing Rockhouse Creek, you'll reach the Cable Trail on the left at 0.2 mile.

Cable Trail

Description: Turn left off the Paw Paw Trail on the Cable Trail and walk a few yards to the drop into Cane Creek Gorge. You must use caution as you descend this very steep chute and maneuver down smooth-faced boulders. A cable is provided to help in your descent.

Once at the bottom, skirt to the right of a large boulder balancing a majestic hemlock tree and step out into the plunge basin of Cane Creek Falls, which tumbles over the stone wall ahead. Around to the left, the more delicate Rockhouse Falls forms a slender ribbon of water on its long drop into the pool.

Climb back up the chute and retrace your steps back to the parking area, or if you want to continue on the Paw Paw Loop, turn left at the trail junction.

26 | LOWER CANE CREEK OVERNIGHT LOOP

Distance: 12.4-mile loop
Difficulty: Moderate
Elevation Change: 760 ft
Cautions: Creek crossings, steep descent and ascent
Connections: Upper Cane Creek Overnight Loop, Paw Paw
Loop, Fall Creek Falls Trail, Gorge Overlook/Woodland
Loop, Cable Trail

Attractions: The lower overnight loop takes you into the depths of Cane Creek Gorge and provides plenty of opportunity for hiking away from the crowds. Camping is available on the east side of the gorge at Campsite 1 and on the west side of the gorge at Campsite 2. If you are backpacking, you must obtain a permit at the park nature center. Even if you're not camping, the park recommends that for your own safety you sign up before hiking one of the overnight loops.

Trailhead: Just inside the north entrance to the state park off TN 30, turn east into a maintenance area and drive past the main building on your right to parking on the left; you'll see a sign for the overnight trails. Walk into the woods to where a connector trail joins the two overnight loops. To the east lies the Upper Cane Creek Overnight Loop (Hike 27). Turn to the west to walk the Lower Cane Creek Overnight Loop.

Description: Head west, following the white blazes. Cross the paved road on which you entered the park. The trail joins the Paw Paw Loop (Hike 24) at 0.4 mile. Turn right; the return will be along the Paw Paw Loop from the left. The trail crosses Paw Paw Creek on a footbridge. Then at 0.5 mile, the overnight trail turns to the right, leaving the Paw Paw Loop.

The trail crosses an old road a couple of times and then descends to cross a creek on a footbridge at 1.1 miles. Across the top of the plateau, the trail descends to cross Walling Mill Creek on a footbridge at 2.3 miles. You'll then join an old logging road and turn left to ascend to Campsite 1 at 2.5 miles. Passing through the camp, the trail turns left off the logging road; just down the trail, you'll find a water well with a hand pump on the right.

At 2.7 miles the trail crosses a creek on stepping stones. At 3.0 miles, approach the rim of Cane Creek Gorge. The trail then descends steeply several hundred feet to Cane Creek; cross the creek on a suspension bridge at

Piney Creek Falls

4.1 miles and then ascend the other side of the gorge. This descent and ascent are difficult sections of the trail; they are steep and have rough footing.

As the trail nears the top of the plateau, a side trail on the left leads to a small waterfall. At 5.0 miles the trail tops out on the plateau and leads to Campsite 2, which also has a well with a hand pump. At the campsite, turn left on a logging road, and then the trail turns left off the road. Cross a small stream on a footbridge and then drop to Piney Creek at 7.0 miles. The trail crosses Piney Creek on the suspension bridge upstream from Piney Creek Falls, which is on the scenic drive. The 85-foot waterfall is in transition between a cascade and a waterfall; the creek drops off a lip of rock to splash into boulders halfway and cascade down the remaining height.

As you ascend from Piney Creek, bear right just before you get to the parking area. From here the overnight trail parallels the road to Piney Creek Falls; keep straight where another path crosses the trail. At 7.4 miles, bear left to cross the road and enter a pine woods. At 7.7 miles is a junction with a side trail left that leads a quarter mile to Millikans Overlook on the scenic drive connecting Fall Creek Falls with Piney Creek Falls. Continuing on the main trail, cross several small streams that may be dry in summer. As you approach the Fall Creek Falls area, cross the trace of an old road no longer used and then emerge onto the paved road at 8.6 miles. The trail crosses the road and reenters the woods to pass below the parking area and connect with the Woodland Trail at 8.7 miles. Turn right on the Woodland Trail (Hike 23) to reach the bridge above Cane Creek Cascade behind the nature center at 9.5 miles. In front of the nature center, pick up the Paw Paw Loop and walk it for half a mile to the loop junction and stay right to close the overnight loop at 12.0 miles and walk the short trail back to the parking area.

27 | Upper Cane Creek Overnight Loop

Distance: 13.7-mile loop
Difficulty: Strenuous
Elevation Change: 240 ft
Cautions: Creek crossings, overgrown sections
Connections: Lower Cane Creek Overnight Loop

Attractions: On the upper end of Cane Creek Gorge, you'll travel through a remote area of the park that is a wildlife management area. Camping is available at Campsite 3. If you are backpacking, you must obtain a permit at the park nature center. Even if you're not camping, the park recommends that for your own safety you sign up before hiking one of the overnight loops.

Trailhead: Just inside the north entrance to the state park off TN 30, turn east into a maintenance area and drive past the main building on your right to parking on the left; you'll see a sign for the overnight trails. Walk into the woods to where a connector trail joins the two overnight loops. To the west lies the Lower Cane Creek Overnight Loop (Hike 26). Turn east to walk the Upper Cane Creek Overnight Loop.

The upper loop can get overgrown with vines and brush, the trail occasionally narrows, and you must keep an eye on the white blazes to stay with the path. So you may want to hike this trail in winter. Be aware that hunting occurs in the wildlife management area east of the main road and south of Fire Tower Road; check with the park staff to determine the hunting schedule.

Description: From the junction of the two overnight loops, turn right. Along the trail, cross two drainages on footbridges and reach an old fence on the left at 0.3 mile where the trail drops to cross a roadbed. The trail then passes through a forest of mixed pine and hardwoods. At 0.5 mile, descend into a more evergreen area of hemlock and laurel to cross

Rockhouse Creek on a bridge. Then crossing a small creek, walk up to the junction of the loop part of the trail at 0.7 mile. Turn right to hike the trail counterclockwise.

The trail moves up and down as it crosses the drainage of the landscape; the low areas may be wet in rainy weather. At 1.7 miles, the trail emerges onto the main park road at the turnoff for the gravel Fire Tower Road. Walk across the paved road, watching for the white blazes on the other side. After passing through a low area with a large patch of groundpine club moss to the left, walk under a powerline at 2.1 miles. The trail descends through switchbacks to ford a tributary of Cane Creek at 3.5 miles. Then at 4.6 miles, descend to hop across a small creek and walk up to the road; cross Cane Creek on the highway bridge. There's a small picnic area where you can run a car shuttle if you want to just do a day hike to this point.

On the other side of the bridge, the trail turns back into the woods on the left. The way is not marked, but watch for a metal pole sticking up at a culvert and you'll see a path leading into the woods; watch for the white blazes. Join an old road to the right for a few paces and then turn left off the road. The trail passes through a low area with ferns littering the forest floor and then turns right out to an old road that is part of the Chinquapin Ridge Mountain Bike Trail at 5.4 miles. Turn left on the road to cross Meadow Creek on a bridge and then turn left off the road soon after. Step across a small creek and then ascend a hill.

At 6.5 miles is Campsite 3, which is the only overnight campsite on the Upper Loop. A side trail to the left leads down to Cane Creek, where you can get water for camping. Curve left and ascend when leaving the campsite.

The trail eventually reaches the edge of Cane Creek, where it turns right to access a suspension bridge at 7.5 miles that takes you over the creek. Stay to the left on the far side of the bridge; do not turn right on the path beside the creek. After several small creek crossings, the trail crosses an old road at 8.1 miles.

Cross more small streams and pass through a scrub forest before dropping to cross some drainages, then cross Flat Rock Branch on a couple of footbridges at 9.5 miles. The trail crosses an old road and reaches a ford of Flat Rock Branch at 9.6 miles. Ascend steeply and cross the creek a couple more times as the trail moves upstream. The trail crosses old roads at 10.4 miles and 10.6 miles and the trace of an old road at 10.9 miles.

The trail enters a pine forest with a carpet of partridgeberry. Cross more small streams and old roads to reach Fire Tower Road at 12.0 miles. The trail leads across the road and eventually closes the loop at 13.0 miles. It's then 0.7 mile back to the parking area.

Map 4. Cumberland Mountain State Rustic Park and Surrounding Area

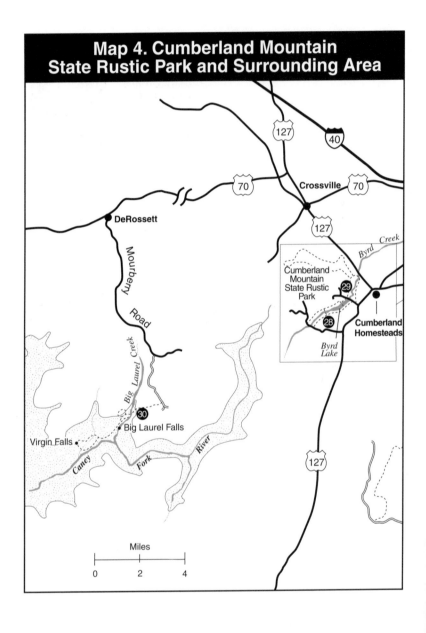

127
40
70 Crossville 70
DeRossett
127
Byrd Creek
Mourberry Road
Cumberland Mountain State Rustic Park
29
Cumberland Homesteads
28
Byrd Lake
Big Laurel Creek
30
Big Laurel Falls
Virgin Falls
Caney Fork River
127

Miles
0   2   4

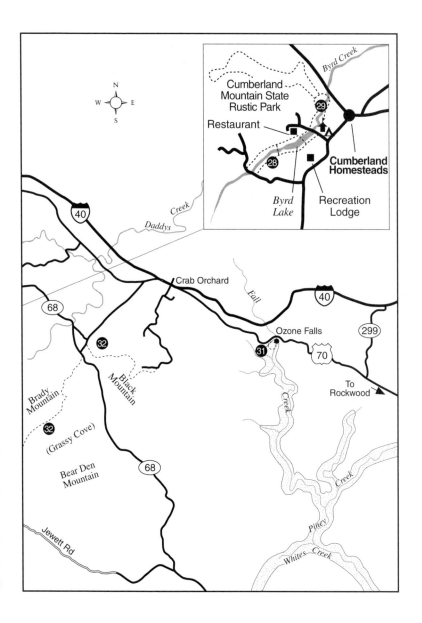

CUMBERLAND MOUNTAIN STATE RUSTIC PARK AND SURROUNDING AREA

On the northern part of the South Cumberland lies Cumberland Mountain State Rustic Park, once the recreational park for the historic Cumberland Homesteads, a New Deal community constructed during the 1930s Depression to provide homes and jobs for those out of work. Today, the park provides opportunities for hiking and enjoying the outdoors of the South Cumberland. Trails circle Byrd Lake, created by a stone dam constructed by the CCC, and penetrate the backcountry along Byrd Creek. The state park has cabins and a campground for overnight stays. Nearby Virgin Falls Pocket Wilderness, Ozone Falls State Natural Area, and the Grassy Cove section of the Cumberland Trail are special places not to be missed.

To get to the park from the north, take Exit 317 off I-40 and head south on US 127 through Crossville. At 7.7 miles, bear right at the Homesteads Tower, now a museum. At 8.4 miles, turn right into the park. From the south, head north on US 127 and climb out of Sequatchie Valley, then drive 9.0 miles until you get to the Homesteads Community; turn left into the park.

28 | PIONEER SHORT LOOP/PIONEER TRAIL

Distance: 5.0-mile loop (Pioneer Short Loop 2.0 miles)
Difficulty: Easy
Elevation Change: 60 ft
Cautions: Creek crossings
Connections: Byrd Lake Trail

Attractions: While circling Byrd Lake, this laurel- and rhododendron-lined loop crosses the lake's numerous contributing streams. The Pioneer Short Loop provides a shorter walk than the longer loop of the Pioneer Trail.

Trailhead: Traveling through Cumberland Mountain State Rustic Park, pass the campground on the right and then the visitor center, also on the right. Cross the old stone dam that holds back Byrd Lake, and then turn left. Pass the park restaurant, turn left again, and pull into the parking area above the lake's boat dock at 0.6 mile from the park entrance off US 127.

Description: From the parking area, walk down to the dock and cross a bridge over Byrd Lake, named for one leader of the Homesteads project. On the other side, the Byrd Lake Trail (Hike 29) with orange blazes bears left. A stairway leads up to the swimming pool and recreation lodge. Turn right and follow the white blazes to hike the Pioneer Short Loop. Follow the water's edge on your right through a pine and laurel forest with occasional fern-capped sandstone boulders and rock shelves to your left.

The pine and laurel give way to rhododendron and hemlock. At 1.0 mile, bear left up stone steps, then watch for a right turn that drops to a cable bridge across Byrd Creek above the lake. This is the optional return by way of the Pioneer Short Loop; circling back at this point makes a 2.0-mile walk.

For a longer hike, continue straight on the Pioneer Trail on a path through an evergreen forest. The way is now marked with green blazes. Bearing left, you'll soon encounter a side stream running past in search of Byrd Creek. At 1.2 miles, step on stones to cross this creek. Loop back right and then left along the moss-lined trail, soon to pick up and cross another side stream.

At 1.8 miles, pass through large hemlocks, bear left through a narrow boulder passageway, and step out into a tall stand of rhododendron, blooming shades of pink in late spring. After crossing a third side stream, walk along Byrd Creek and pass through a sandstone corridor before the trail bears left and climbs to join a paved road at 3.0 miles. This is the Old Mail Road. Turn right on the road to cross the stone bridge over Byrd Creek, and then turn right again, off the road, dropping into the woods on the other side of the creek to return toward the center of the park.

Gently ascend through a predominantly pine forest. Then descend to cross a side creek at 3.8 miles and double back right down the small creek for a short distance before swinging left to parallel Byrd Creek again.

At 4.0 miles, reconnect with the Pioneer Short Loop; the green blazes lead to your right to the bridge across Byrd Creek. Stay straight, following the white blazes. At 4.5 miles, a rock slab over the lake's edge offers a lazy lunch spot. Approach the park cabins. After passing below the cabins, the trail returns to the parking area for the boat dock.

29 | BYRD LAKE, CUMBERLAND PLATEAU, AND BYRD CREEK TRAILS

Distance: 4.0-mile loop
Difficulty: Easy
Elevation Change: 60 ft
Cautions: Stream crossings, rocky descent
Connections: Pioneer Short Loop, Cumberland Overnight Trail

Attractions: This pleasant, easy walk swings around Byrd Lake, passes over the park's old stone dam, and follows Byrd Creek below the dam into

Cumberland Mountain Park Dam

a luxuriant forest of hemlock and rhododendron. This is the best route for viewing the dam, the largest steel-free masonry structure undertaken by the CCC.

Trailhead: Pass the Cumberland Mountain State Rustic Park Visitor Center on the right, cross the old stone dam that holds back Byrd Lake, and then turn left. Pass the park restaurant, turn left again, and pull into the parking area above the lake's boat dock at 0.6 mile from the park entrance off US 127. From the parking area, walk down to the boat dock. You can also access this trail system from the visitor center or the park restaurant.

Description: From the boat dock, cross Byrd Lake on the bridge to the other side, where the Pioneer Short Loop (Hike 28) turns right and the paved steps straight ahead lead up to the swimming pool. Turn left to walk the orange-blazed Byrd Lake Trail. Along the lake shore, at 0.2 mile, the trail ascends along a small tributary, but then turns left to drop and cross the stream on stepping stones. Step over another stream as the trail continues along the lake to ascend to the road at the park dam at 0.7 mile. You could park at the visitor center to the right and join the trail at this location. Turn left along the road over the dam. On the other side, you're not far from the restaurant to the left, so you could also park there and join the hike on this west side of the dam.

On the right side of the road, you'll see the 1.0-mile Cumberland Plateau Trail heading into the woods; this is the way you'll return if you're hiking a shorter loop. Turn right down steps beside the dam; the trail is steep and rocky. Hike to the bottom of the dam beside Byrd Creek, which spills down from the arch openings in the dam. On the other side of the creek sits the group lodge, the Old Stone Mill House, one of the original structures of the Homesteads Project, originally intended as a mill but never used.

To continue, bear left, paralleling the creek downstream from the dam and passing through a wood of hemlock, white pine, laurel, and rhododendron while following the red blazes of the Cumberland Plateau Trail. At 0.8 mile, rockhop a small tributary stream and then climb to pass under a powerline at 0.9 mile.

The trail descends to streamside at 1.0 mile. Stay along the creek to a junction at 1.2 miles with the Byrd Creek Trail. You can turn left here to complete the Cumberland Plateau Trail and reemerge on the road at the dam in a half mile. To hike a longer loop, stay straight on the 2.1-mile Byrd Creek Trail, following the yellow blazes. The trail parallels Byrd Creek, lazily floating downstream from the dam amid rhododendron.

Cross a couple of small drainages before the trail moves away from the creek and crosses a stream using stepping stones to ascend to a junction with the Cumberland Overnight Trail at 1.8 miles. This 6-mile trail, sporadically marked with blue blazes, is mostly level as it wanders through a second-growth forest and then loops back across moss-covered sandstone slabs to rejoin the Byrd Creek Trail after crossing Threemile Creek on a bridge.

To stay on the Byrd Creek Trail, bear right at the Overnight Trail intersection and continue following the yellow blazes to 1.9 miles, where the Overnight Trail rejoins after making its long loop. Just beyond this second junction, the Byrd Creek Trail intersects with an old paved road below US 127. Turn right on this road and cross Byrd Creek on the old road bridge.

Just after the bridge, turn right into the woods into a low area; bear left and then right. The trail curves right to drop and cross a small creek at 2.5 miles. Soon after, you'll be back at Byrd Creek. At 3.1 miles, the trail crosses a creek on stepping stones. Parallel a powerline and at 3.2 miles turn left to cross the open area under the line. The trail then ascends, makes a turn left, and continues up to pass the campground through the trees to your left and finally emerge onto the parking lot for the visitor center at 3.3 miles. In front of the visitor center, you can reconnect with the Byrd Lake Trail to the right to get back to the boat dock, or for a shorter walk, you can turn right along the road across the dam and then left to follow the road to the parking area for the boat dock.

30 | VIRGIN FALLS POCKET WILDERNESS

Distance: 4.0 miles one way
Difficulty: Moderate
Elevation Loss: 800 ft
Cautions: Creek crossings, caged ladders, unmarked
    sections
Connections: None

Attractions: This is one of the most interesting trails on the South Cumberland, with overlooks and waterfalls, including the dramatic 110-foot Virgin Falls. Here a robust stream emerges from a cave and crashes over a cliff into a pit, sending spray up the hillside before it disappears into the earth. Camping is available beside the Caney Fork River.

Trailhead: To the west of Cumberland Mountain State Rustic Park lies Virgin Falls Pocket Wilderness, the first pocket wilderness set aside by Bowater Incorporated from their timber lands. East of Sparta and west of Crossville on US 70 in DeRossett, turn south on Mourberry Road, marked by a small pocket wilderness sign. At 5.9 miles turn right on the gravel Scott Gulf Road for another 2.0 miles to the trailhead on the right. Adjacent to the pocket wilderness, Scott Gulf recently was donated to the state and is now managed by the Tennessee Wildlife Resources Agency. Watch for new hiking trails to be developed in the area.

Description: Just to the right of the parking area entrance, begin your hike across the plateautop through second-growth timber. At 0.5 mile, a creek on your right leads through a laurel thicket, and at 0.8 mile the trail descends; make a stepping-stone creek crossing and descend again. Watch for a spur trail on the left leading to Big Branch Falls, where the creek skips down a stone staircase.

Continue to descend on the main trail for a short distance, bearing right and then crossing Big Laurel Creek on flat boulders. At a fork at 1.5 miles, a trail left descends along Big Laurel Creek and rejoins the main trail above Big Laurel Falls. The main trail leads to the right, marked with an occasional white blaze. Ascend on wooden steps with a sandstone bluff to your right. In winter, with leaves off the trees, you can see the Caney Fork River Valley to the south. At 1.8 miles is a junction with the Caney Fork Overlook loop. The trail right takes you up caged ladders to a flat-rock overlook offering a stone bench for a rest while you enjoy the sweeping view of the valley. From the overlook, walk along the bluff, bearing left in front of the blazed tree. Switchback left and descend on a steep caged ladder to complete the loop. Turn right on the main trail and descend to a junction with the other end of the creekside alternative route.

Descend right, following Big Laurel Creek on your left until it falls 30 feet off a rock shelter lip and disappears into a sinkhole. The trail drops to a level with the falls, where a spur trail left leads to the base of Big Laurel Falls. The main trail turns right.

Continue west on the main trail along the side of a steep bluff where the

Virgin Falls

Big Laurel Falls in Virgin Falls Pocket Wilderness

Caney Fork appears through the trees below to your left just before the beginning of the Virgin Falls Loop at 3.0 miles. At the loop junction, turn right along a fragmented limestone wall.

At 3.4 miles is Sheep Cave, where a slender stream emerges from the cave high up the bluff, bounces and falls in a steep descent, and drops into a limestone sink below. A steep spur trail right leads up to the cave mouth.

The main trail turns left to cross a ravine that's the main drainage for Little Laurel Creek, dry most of the time. Climb a ridge and descend to face thundering Virgin Falls, which sails over a cliff into a sinkhole, at 4.0 miles.

A spur trail climbs to the right, circling the falls, to cross over the stream just where it glides from the mouth of a cave and flows 50 feet over a smooth rock surface before dropping over the side of the cliff. Use caution and expect slippery rocks.

From the base of the falls, continue the Virgin Falls Loop by descending south, down a ravine, and crossing Little Laurel Creek to a junction where a trail sign sends you left on the main trail. Right leads to a camp area near the Caney Fork River. To the left, climb through a maze of boulders and follow the ridge to complete the loop. The way is not well marked, so keep an eye on the path. At the loop junction, turn to the right back to Big Laurel Falls and then to the junction with the overlook trail to the left. Stay right along the creekside alternative for the shortest return.

31 OZONE FALLS STATE NATURAL AREA

Distance: 0.25 mile one way
Difficulty: Moderate
Elevation Loss: 100 ft
Cautions: High bluff; steep, rocky descent
Connections: None

Attractions: At the end of this short trail is a narrow 110-foot column of water falling from a rock overhang. The amphitheater behind the water-

fall is typical of waterfalls on the Cumberland Plateau, where below the erosion-resistant sandstone lip of the falls, the softer sandstone and shale layers erode more quickly, opening up the rock wall behind the fall of water.

Trailhead: Ozone Falls State Natural Area lies to the east of Cumberland Mountain StatePark.From Crossville, take US 70 east, passing through the community of Crab Orchard and then continuing another 4.5 miles to Ozone. Or on I-40 from either the east or the west, take Exit 338 at Westel Road just east of Crab Orchard and drive south on

Ozone Falls

TN 299 2.8 miles to US 70 and turn right for 4.4 miles to Ozone. The state natural area lies in the small community of Ozone, named for the "stimulating quality of the air." Watch for a sign for the natural area on the south side of the road.

Description: Before taking the trail to the base of the falls, walk the short path to the left of the natural area sign to the top of the waterfall, where Fall Creek slides through a narrow chute and leaps beyond the supporting sandstone bluff into the gorge below. There are no safety rails along the bluff's edge, so take care.

The trail to the base of the falls leads to the right of the natural area sign, paralleling the road. Or from the top of the falls, take a path to the right along the gorge rim; the two paths converge. At 0.1 mile a stone wall at the edge of the highway signals a left turn where the trail descends into the small gorge; there's room to park one car if you want to start your walk here. Soon after you begin the rocky descent, there's a fork in the path. Straight ahead along the rock wall will take you to views of the waterfall pouring into a blue-green pool. Right down the slope will take you below the plunge pool of the waterfall, where if there's plenty of water, a cascade from the pool dances down the creek.

32 | CUMBERLAND TRAIL (GRASSY COVE SECTION)

Distance: 11.7 miles one way
Difficulty: Moderate
Elevation Change: 1,200 ft
Cautions: Creek crossings, mudholes, road crossings
Connections: None

Attractions: From the Black Mountain state-registered natural area, where massive rock formations create a maze of passages, the Cumberland Trail follows the ridgeline of Black Mountain and Brady Mountain for distant views of Grassy Cove. You may camp along the trail, but no campfires are allowed.

In 1968 a group of hikers and conservationists organized the Tennessee Trails Association (TTA) and proposed a trans-Tennessee trail that would pass north to south through the state, following the eastern edge of the Cumberland Plateau. At first, the Tennessee General Assembly supported the idea by establishing the Cumberland Trail, a state scenic trail that would have run 200 miles from Cumberland Gap National Historical Park on the Kentucky border to Chattanooga near the Georgia–Alabama border. For a time, the state of Tennessee abandoned the trail for lack of funds. In the late 1990s the TTA organized a Cumberland Trail Conference with the

Springhouse

mission of reopening the Cumberland Trail. The conference was so successful in organizing public support and getting volunteers to work on the trail that in 1998 the state established a new Cumberland Trail State Park. Segments of the trail are under construction by volunteers. At this writing this Grassy Cove section and a section at Prentice Cooper to the south are the only segments on the South Cumberland. Eventually, the trail will connect these segments.

Trailhead: At the Crab Orchard Exit off I-40, between Crossville on the west and Westel Road on the east, turn south 0.3 mile to a T-junction. To the left is a dead end. Turn right, and the road soon curves left. In 1.8 miles turn left on Owl Roost Road to ascend Black Mountain. At 2.5 miles, enter the Black Mountain State Natural Area, owned by the Methodist Church. Pass a communication tower to the right and, at 4.5 miles, turn in at a road to the left; the road is not in good shape, so you may want to park here and walk in. Pass a pullout on the right and at 0.1 mile turn right on a side road leading up to an old housesite. You'll see a chimney up to the right and straight ahead a springhouse where the trail begins.

To run a shuttle, you'll need to leave a car where the trail currently ends on Jewett Road off TN 68 south of Grassy Cove.

Description: To begin the Grassy Cove section of the Cumberland Trail, you will take the path up the bank to the right of the springhouse. But before proceeding, you may want to explore the massive rock formations for which the area is known. Stay on the road to the left of the springhouse, crossing the little stream that runs from the spring, and watch for a trail to the right just before another old house site with standing chimney. The side path leads into a maze of house-size blocks of sandstone. At one location, you can climb to the top for distant views of Grassy Cove, but take care.

Back at the springhouse, turn up the Cumberland Trail, marked with white blazes. The trail veers to the left on an old road and follows it up across the top of the mountain. At 0.1 mile, the trail veers left off the road, and at 0.3 mile it passes a path to the right that leads to a communication tower standing at the end of the road you drove up the mountain. Then at 0.4 mile the trail turns left and drops along stairs wedged between massive boulders. The trail then passes between huge rocks and turns left again. It travels through another passageway and then heads down through a brier patch, crosses a jeep road, and hits an old roadbed.

Turn right and follow the roadbed through second-growth forest until at 0.8 mile the trail turns right off the road and begins descending. At 1.0 mile the trail follows an old roadbed along the west slope of Black Mountain. At 1.5 miles the trail bears left for a steep descent, leaving the old road.

The trail bottoms out in a gap at a junction of roads. Go straight ahead and ascend the other side of the gap. The trail bears left and follows the ridgeline until at 2.2 miles a steep descent takes you down to an old road. Turn left for 50 feet to a junction of roads. Turn right. From here the trail gradually descends along the hollow of Clear Branch.

At 3.0 miles the trail crosses Clear Branch and follows along the right side. In late summer, watch for cardinal flower. Cross the branch three more times and walk along the left side of the creek. Cross the creek again and follow along the right side, crossing side creeks along the way. At 4.0 miles emerge onto the paved Cox's Valley Road. Turn left and walk along the road to TN 68 at 4.4 miles. Turn left again until at 4.8 miles the trail crosses the highway to a parking area, where the trail begins a climb up Brady Mountain.

The trail ascends along an old road for half a mile and then continues on the road until at 5.8 miles the trail enters Low Gap. Turn left, walk 100 feet, and turn up a road to the right that makes a steep ascent.

At 6.4 miles the trail follows the ridgeline and then climbs steeply through boulders around a rock outcropping. The trail continues along the ridgeline to another outcropping, where you'll have glimpses of Grassy Cove to the east. To the west is Cumberland Homesteads, which you can see through the trees in winter.

Below where you stand, Mill Cave drains Grassy Cove. Part of the Sequatchie Valley system, the cove is a depression in the plateau, a valley of gracefully rolling farmland. The cove is completely surrounded by mountains, with Black, Brady, and Bear Den Mountains in a somewhat triangular shape. The main drainage in the cove, Cove Creek, travels from the southwest and empties into Mill Cave at the base of Brady Mountain. The water emerges on the west side of Brady Mountain as the headwaters of the Sequatchie River. This is typical of karst formations (limestone regions with sinks, caves, and underground streams). The unusual geology of Grassy Cove has been recognized by its designation as a National Natural Landmark.

From the Grassy Cove view, the trail wanders across the top of Brady Mountain. The ridgeline is sometimes a flat forested area, other times a narrow rocky ridge. At 8.5 miles, turn left onto an old road.

At 10.5 miles, the trail reaches a gap; turn left on another dirt road that descends steeply. The trail bears left at 10.9 miles and joins another road to the right. At 11.2 miles, the trail drops off the road to the left; the trail is hard to follow here, so watch for the white blazes. Soon the trail crosses a dirt road in Key Reed Gap. Drop through a hollow littered with boulders to Jewett Road, at this point a gravel road, but a paved road where it turns off TN 68 south of Grassy Cove.

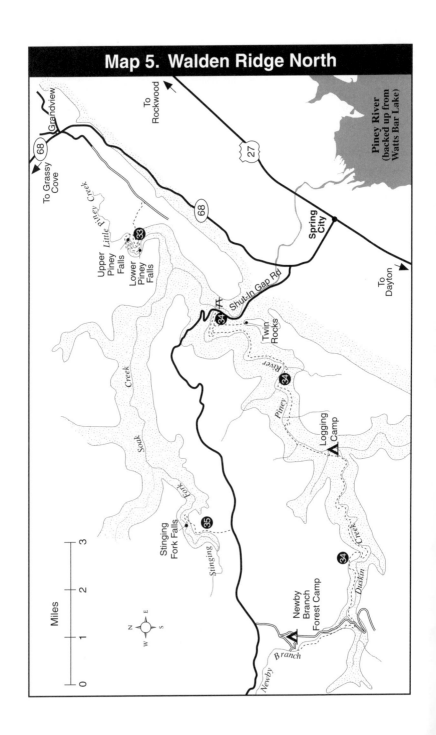

Map 5. Walden Ridge North

WALDEN RIDGE NORTH

Sequatchie Valley divides the South Cumberland northeast to southwest, with most of the Cumberland Plateau to the west and a strip of separated tableland to the east. This long ridge on the east is called Walden Ridge, after an early explorer. While the main part of the plateau has such large preserves as Savage Gulf State Natural Area and Fall Creek Falls State Park, Walden Ridge has several smaller enclaves, but ones that are just as interesting and challenging for hikers and backpackers. Trails lead to numerous waterfalls on the northern half and past overlooks of the Tennessee River Gorge on the lower section. To the east, below the Cumberland Plateau, lies the Valley and Ridge Province, locally called the Great Valley of East Tennessee.

The trails here are described north to south. To get to the northern end of the Walden Ridge section of the South Cumberland, take TN 68 southeast from the Cumberland Homesteads and Cumberland Mountain State Park. The highway travels through Grassy Cove, separated from Sequatchie Valley by Brady Mountain. Ascending from Grassy Cove, the road mounts Walden Ridge. If you are coming from the south, take US 27, which parallels the eastern wall of the plateau, northeast to Spring City, and then take TN 68 north up the plateau.

33 | PINEY FALLS STATE NATURAL AREA

Distance: 0.7-mile loop (1.7 miles with the access road)
Difficulty: Moderate
Elevation Change: 160 ft
Cautions: Difficult climb, steep dropoffs, creek ford
Connections: None

Attractions: The Upper Piney Falls Loop provides access to two major waterfalls in the Piney Falls State Natural Area on the northern part of Walden Ridge.

Trailhead: From the Cumberland Mountain State Park/Cumberland Homesteads, take TN 68 southeast to Grandview on Walden Ridge. From the south, take US 27 northeast to Spring City, and then take TN 68 north, up the plateau, to Grandview. Turn south at a sign for Piney Falls. At 1.5 miles down this road, which becomes gravel, there's a dirt road on the right. The natural area is a half mile down this dirt road, which is not suitable for

Upper Piney Falls

passenger cars. Unless you have four-wheel drive, park here along the road and walk in, which will add a half mile each way to your walk.

Description: The road drops to a wet-weather stream crossing and then ascends to pass over a ridge. When you get to a right fork on the ridge, stay left on the main road; the right fork is becoming overgrown. Drop to pass through a clearing under a power line. The road drops again through a hollow, leads up to enter the natural area and, at 0.5 mile, reaches the trailhead at a loop junction.

You can hike the loop either way, but the best approach is clockwise. Stay to the left, still on the dirt road until it ends, and then follow the white-blazed trail into the woods to the right. Begin dropping below the bluff line; if there is much water in Little Piney Creek, you'll hear the lower waterfall in the gorge on your left. At 0.6 mile the trail switchbacks left and soon after curves back right as it makes its descent, stepping down a rock shelf. As the trail curves around a rock bluff to the right, you'll be above Lower Piney Falls. There is no established side trail to the falls, but at this location you can make your way down the steep slope to stand at the top of the falls, where the creek drops 50 feet into a rock-walled plunge basin; use caution along the edge. The water prepares for its leap by first skipping down a 10-foot cascade above the falls.

Back on the established trail, follow along the rock bluff while passing upstream along Little Piney Creek, which is below on your left. The trail passes along the bluff to Upper Piney Falls at 0.7 mile. This waterfall plunges 80 feet over a lip of rock and splashes into rock at the bottom before flowing into a pool. At times of high water, it's quite a rush of water.

The trail passes behind the waterfall and circles around to pass downstream for a short distance, climbing and passing along the rock bluff. At 0.8 mile the trail turns up the rock bluff where you must climb from ledge to ledge; take your time and be careful. It's not particularly dangerous, but use caution if the rocks are wet or icy. Unfortunately, this turn up the rock bluff was not marked, and hikers missing the turn had made a path straight ahead; ignore it. Watch for two large hemlocks forming a V at ground level as a marker for where the trail turns up. If you are not up to making the climb, simply return the way you came; the state may reroute the trail to avoid this climb in the future.

At the top of the bluff, the trail turns right and follows the bluff line back toward the upper falls. Short paths to the right take you to overlooks of the falls at the bluff edge. Eventually the trail passes above the falls, and then at 1.0 mile curves back right and drops to a ford of the creek just above the falls. In times of low water, you'll be able to rockhop, but when the water is up, you must ford. You might explore upstream for a better crossing.

Once across, the trail heads up the slope. Stay to the left where another path leads right. Ascend to the trailhead to complete the loop at 1.2 miles. It's then 0.5 mile back along the access road to where you parked.

34 | PINEY RIVER TRAIL

Distance: 10.0 miles one way (Twin Rocks Nature Loop 1.7 miles)
Difficulty: Easy to moderate
Elevation Change: 700 ft
Cautions: Caged ladder, rocky in places, poison ivy
Connections: None

Attractions: The Walden Ridge section of the South Cumberland contains Bowater Inc. forests with hiking trails intended for use by the public. On this loop, located on the Piney River Tree Farm, you can climb atop Twin Rocks for a view east off the plateau and of the Piney River Gorge. Farther on, there are impressive cascades in the river and creeks. Camping is available at the Logging Camp along the trail and at Newby Branch Forest Camp.

Trailhead: From Grandview, head southeast down TN 68. Or from Spring City on US 27, turn northwest on TN 68 and at 1.4 miles turn left on Shut-In Gap Road. The Piney River Picnic Area and parking lie on the right in another 1.2 miles. If you want to run a shuttle, drop a vehicle at the Newby Branch Forest Camp at the other end. The camp has a water pump, tables, and pit toilets, and can be reached by continuing on Shut-In Gap Road 5.9 miles beyond the Piney River picnic area.

Description: From the picnic area, walk across the road and up the hill to the trailhead signs. The trail leads into the woods a short distance to your right. Just into the woods, begin the Twin Rocks Nature Loop by turning left at a junction. The main trail straight ahead is blazed with a hiker in a green disk; spur trails, like this side loop, are blazed with a hiker in a blue disk.

On the Twin Rocks Nature Loop, climb through a forest of mixed hardwoods and up steps to a junction at 0.3 mile. Turn left on a spur trail to Twin Rocks at 0.6 mile. Bear right around the rock monoliths and then swing to the left and climb between the Twin Rocks on a caged ladder for a high overlook. The view is east off the plateau and reveals Piney River as it meanders around the ridge on its journey to join the Tennessee River.

Back on the main trail is a junction at 1.2 miles. If you're just out to complete the Twin Rocks Nature Loop, turn right at this junction. Along this return route, a side trail to the left leads to the Flat Rock picnic area on the Piney River; the trail then follows the river back to the trailhead and parking area for a total of 1.7 miles.

At the junction with the return route, turn left to continue on the Piney River Trail, following Piney River upstream while walking high above the river. This next section of trail is great for wildflowers in spring. Descend to a junction at 2.4 miles with a side trail right that leads 0.1 mile down to Dead End Bend on the river. Continue straight on the main trail.

Soon after, the trail

Piney River Crossing

crosses a rock shelf below a low overhang, passes dripping walls, and ducks under another overhang at 2.8 miles. Pass through a couple of dry drainages and then cross a stream where the water trickles off the rock ledge to your left in a thousand rivulets. At 3.0 miles, rockhop McDonald Branch, a large stream that falls through great slabs of rock, a good site for lunch. The trail then crosses several small drainages and boulder-strewn sections, turning right and descending to a suspension bridge over Piney River at 4.2 miles. There's a great swimming hole downstream of the bridge.

On the other side, turn left to follow the river upstream on an old narrow-gauge railroad bed that was used for lumber and coal operations. At 4.4 miles, the trail brushes against a rock wall spotted with blooming saxifrage in spring. At 4.5 miles, cross Pine Branch on a bridge; notice Pine Branch Falls upstream. At 5.0 miles, the trail reaches Rockhouse Branch; the rock foundations remain from a bridge that once carried the narrow-gauge train across the creek. Turn right upstream to cross the branch on a bridge; notice on the right the "bathtub" created by water spilling into a rock depression. Turn left downstream to a junction at 5.1 miles with the Logging Camp Loop. You can stay right on the main trail or descend on the left fork to a campsite on the river. If you head this way, descend to the old railroad bed (ignore an old sign that directs you left, if it's still there); turn right on the railroad bed to get back to the main trail.

The upper part of the loop passes a spur trail to the right that once led to a campsite, now abandoned. The upper and lower trails come back together at 5.3 miles.

The trail now turns up Duskin Creek, climbing a path above the old railroad bed. At 5.8 miles, descend left to creekside. Watch for a spur trail to the left just before reaching the creek; the trail leads 0.1 mile to Hemlock Falls, a broad, low falls on Duskin Creek. On the main trail at creekside, turn right to continue upstream.

At 6.0 miles, the trail ascends to a bridge over a side pool of the creek. To your left, in the main channel of the creek, you'll see Deep Pool Cascades. Beyond, at 6.1 miles, the creek forms an impressive cascade as you enter Big Cove. The trail swings through Big Cove and ascends and then curves right to continue up Duskin Creek.

There's a spur trail to Spider Den Bluff on the left at 6.7 miles as the main trail turns right; the side trail descends steeply 0.2 mile to creekside, where the stream flows below tall bluffs. At 7.2 miles, the trail drops to creek level again. Watch for a layered rock up to the right and, just beyond, White Pine Cascades.

Begin an ascent of the slope with a switchback right. At 7.7 miles, the trail passes an old mine site to the right. Soon after, turn down to the creek again and continue upstream, often in the floodplain; notice more cascades and spillways in the creek. The trail heads up to a switchback right and then a curve left; at 8.4 miles, cross Duskin Creek on a bridge. The trail now wanders out to a road at 8.8 miles. Turn right on the road and cross a bridge back over Duskin Creek. The trail turns left off the road back into the woods. The trail then turns right and ascends the slope, eventually turning left through boulders and following Newby Branch upstream. Cross a dry creek on stones, now following an old roadbed. At 9.9 miles, the trail crosses a bridge over Newby Branch and ascends to the Newby Branch Forest Camp at 10.0 miles.

35 | STINGING FORK POCKET WILDERNESS

Distance: 1.5 miles one way
Difficulty: Moderate
Elevation Loss: 300 ft
Cautions: Steep descent, rough footing
Connections: None

Attractions: This trail through Bowater's small Stinging Fork Pocket Wilderness descends from the plateautop to the base of a 30-foot fan-shaped waterfall on Stinging Fork Creek. Nearby Newby Branch Forest Camp offers camping.

Trailhead: From Grandview, head southeast down TN 68. Or from Spring City on US 27, turn northwest on TN 68 and at 1.4 miles turn left on Shut-In Gap Road. Past the Piney River Picnic Area and parking on the right for the Piney River Trail (Hike 34) in 1.2 miles, continue on Shut-In Gap Road. In 4.1 miles, Stinging Fork Pocket Wilderness lies on the right. To reach Newby Branch Forest Camp and the west end of the Piney River Trail, continue on Shut-In Gap Road 1.3 miles and turn left on a gravel road, following the "Forest Camp" signs another 0.5 mile to the camp.

Description: Enter the woods just to the left of the pocket wilderness sign and walk through a planted pine forest along a moss-lined trail trimmed with mountain laurel. At 1.0 mile a side trail left leads to Indian Head Point for a view across the gorge and Stinging Fork Creek below.

Continue on the main trail and descend through boulder fields on switchbacks and wooden steps; blue arrows on trees mark the way. Below to the trail's left, Stinging Fork Creek cascades around the bend, then makes its 30-foot fall.

High above the creek, continue downstream along Stinging Fork and then switchback left through river birch and rhododendron to the base of the falls. You'll see Stinging Fork Creek dance down the craggy wall, fanning out for its entry into the pool below.

Retrace your steps, ascending from the gorge bottom to the parking area.

Stinging Fork Falls

Map 6. Laurel – Snow Pocket Wilderness

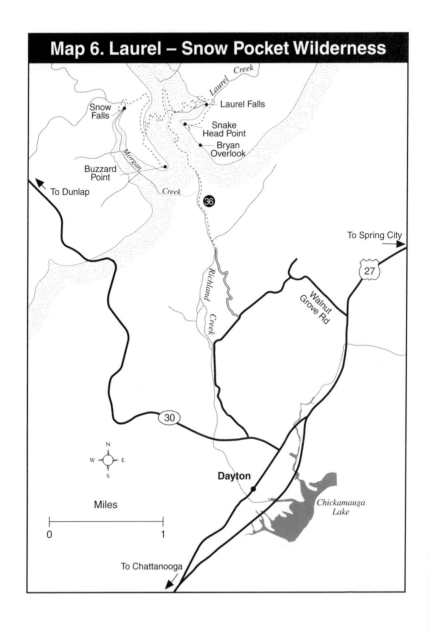

LAUREL–SNOW POCKET WILDERNESS

Belonging to Bowater Inc., a paper company, this pocket wilderness is open to the public. The hiking trail through this state-registered natural area was the first designated national recreation trail in Tennessee. Laurel–Snow Pocket Wilderness is located northwest of Chickamauga Lake on the Tennessee River and the community of Dayton, which was the site of the famous Scopes Monkey Trial that in 1925 challenged the state law against the teaching of evolution.

36 | LAUREL–SNOW POCKET WILDERNESS TRAIL

Distance: 10.5 miles round-trip
Difficulty: Strenuous
Elevation Change: 1,000 ft
Cautions: Creek crossings, boulder passages, two ascents
Connections: None

Attractions: The trail through the Laurel–Snow Pocket Wilderness leads to two waterfalls and two panoramic overlooks of the Great Valley of East Tennessee.

The Richland Creek watershed was once a thriving coal-producing area. Along the trail you'll see remains of the operation, including retaining walls that protected the rail line that ran along the creek bank. More remains of the

Buzzard Point

coal mining operation are located just south of the parking area; a trail leads to rows of coke ovens that stretch through the woods for 200 yards. Unfortunately, they are now overgrown with kudzu and barely recognizable.

Trailhead: Drive to Dayton on US 27, from either the north or the south. Turn west on Walnut Grove Road, directly across from the Rhea County Medical Center on the north end of Dayton. In 0.7 mile, turn left at a Y junction on Black Valley Road. In another 0.7 mile, turn right onto the dirt Richland Creek Road, and in 1.0 mile you'll reach the end of the road and the parking area and trailhead.

Description: The trail gently ascends upstream along Richland Creek, which spills down from the highlands. In the first few hundred yards, cross two wooden bridges, the second supported by old stone piers from a railroad bridge that once carried a coal train.

Just beyond the second bridge, a side path up the bank on your right takes you to a stone arch that probably was part of a bridge to take coal down from the mines above to the main rail line along the creek. Just beyond this side path, you'll find an old air shaft on the right.

At 0.4 mile on the trail, a wet weather stream spills down from the right and splashes across the trail where old railroad ties are exposed. Immediately across Richland Creek, Morgan Creek joins Richland; above you can see the rock bluff of Buzzard Point. At 0.7 mile, the trail crosses another wooden bridge over a ravine, where you'll see what is left of a large pipe that once carried water to Dayton. Afterwards, the main trail switches up right, but you can stay straight ahead for a short walk to the old Dayton Reservoir, where a low dam still stretches across the creek.

On the main trail, climb gradually until the trail crosses Laurel Creek on a metal bridge at 1.4 miles. Bear right through a field of small boulders (the trail is hard to see here) until at 1.5 miles the trail splits, with Laurel Falls to the right and Snow Falls to the left.

Headed to Laurel Falls, ascend through large boulders. At 1.6 miles, a short side trail on the right takes you to the foot of a small cascade. Just beyond the cascade, you must crawl through a hole under some boulders. The trail turns right and then swings left before continuing the ascent of the gorge through three switchbacks. The trail leads to 80-foot Laurel Falls at 2.5 miles, where Laurel Creek spills over the sandstone rim of the gorge.

From the waterfall, you can continue on the trail, switching back to the left, ascending through a break in the gorge rim to the plateautop. The trail then leads back along the rim, eventually crossing Laurel Creek above the falls. You could get your feet wet if the water's up. The trail continues through the woods. At 3.5 miles, pass a jeep road to the left and approach the edge for panoramic views of the gorge of Richland Creek from Bryan Overlook, named for William Jennings Bryan, who prosecuted John Scopes for teaching evolution. To the right is Snake Head Point, a promontory that thrusts out into the gorge for views up and down Richland Creek.

From here you must return to Laurel Falls, descend to where the trail splits, and take the other fork to see Snow Falls. The trail leads through hardwoods and boulder fields; watch for a turn down left and then right across a ledge. Emerge beside Richland Creek, where three metal bridges take you to the other side.

The trail bears left and follows the creek downstream on the other side. Eventually, turn away from the creek and begin a second ascent of the gorge wall through the forest. Watch for a sign indicating that the main trail switches back to the right.

Ascend through boulders, then switchback left and continue the long ascent; it's easy to lose the trail, so keep an eye on where you're going. In winter, with the leaves off the trees, you will see Laurel Falls across the gorge. Near the top, walk along the foot of a cliff wall, then swing right and ascend through a crack in the wall to the top of the plateau at 1.0 mile from the beginning of the Snow Falls section of the trail.

Laurel Falls, Laurel–Snow Pocket Wilderness

The trail turns right and passes along the gorge rim to a quarter-mile side trail, marked by a sign, to Buzzard Point. Turn left for the overlook, then turn left on a jeep road and walk to the road's end, where you will stand on a nearly bare wedge of rock that points down the gorge of Richland Creek to where it opens into the Great Valley of East Tennessee. It's a grand view of the Tennessee River and, on a clear day, the faint Appalachians on the far side of the valley.

Backtrack to the main trail and continue on to Snow Falls. Pass through a pine forest and emerge into a cleared area under a powerline. When you reach a jeep road under the powerline, turn right, and in a few feet turn left back into the woods. The trail eventually turns away from the gorge rim and crosses a jeep road. Descend gradually, bearing left, finally dropping to Morgan Creek. Again you have a creek crossing where you may get your feet wet. In winter, it can be iced over.

On the other side, the trail turns right, soon loops left, crosses an old road, and drops through rocks to the bottom of Snow Falls at 0.5 mile from the side trail to Buzzard Rock. This small waterfall is interesting because it drops about 12 feet to hit a boulder and shoot off at a 45-degree angle. The trail ends at Snow Falls, and from here it's a 3-mile walk back to the parking area.

Map 7. North Chickamauga Pocket Wilderness

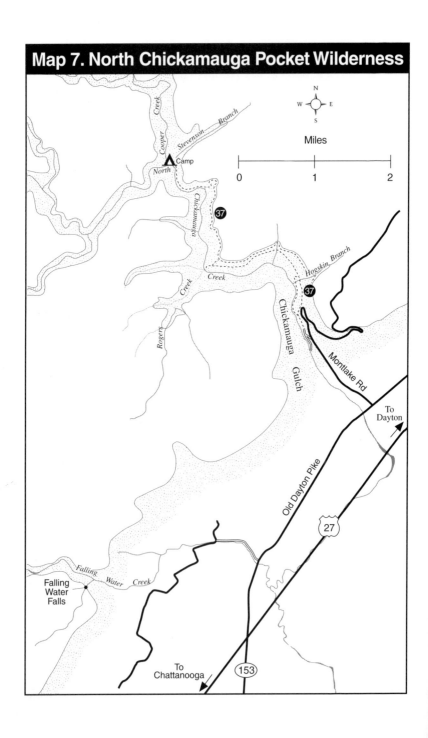

NORTH CHICKAMAUGA POCKET WILDERNESS

The newest of the Bowater Inc. pocket wilderness areas, North Chickamauga Pocket Wilderness protects the gorge of North Chickamauga Creek, a tributary of the Tennessee River. In this state-registered natural area, a short loop and a longer trail lead into the narrow gorge called Chickamauga Gulch. North Chickamauga Pocket Wilderness is located to the northwest of Chattanooga.

37 | STEVENSON BRANCH TRAIL

Distance: 3.9 miles one way (Hogskin Branch Loop 1.5 miles)
Difficulty: Moderate
Elevation Change: 700 ft
Cautions: Creek crossings, rocky path, steep sections
Connections: None

Attractions: The Stevenson Branch Trail penetrates Chickamauga Gulch, a deep cleft in the side of the Cumberland Plateau, and passes by waterfalls, outcrops, and gorge views. There's camping on Stevenson Branch at the end of the trail, and the Hogskin Branch Loop offers a shorter route back to parking.

Trailhead: South along US 27 from Dayton, or 12 miles north from Chattanooga, get off at the TN 153 exit and turn west. You'll then be on the Old Dayton Pike. In 0.6 mile, cross Falling Water Creek. The state has designated a portion of Falling Water Gorge as a state natural area, and there will eventually be a trail that leads to 110-foot Falling Water Falls; the trailhead will be on Levi Road that's just up Roberts Mill Road. Continuing on Old Dayton Pike, at 3.0 miles cross North Chickamauga Creek and turn left on Montlake Road. At 4.0 miles, turn left into the North Chickamauga Pocket Wilderness. Descend on the gravel road to a parking area at 4.1 miles. Walk right on a rough side road to the trailhead in another 0.1 mile.

Description: Walk down an old road into the woods; vehicles are not allowed. A side path left leads below a picnic table to creekside; North Chickamauga Creek runs down Chickamauga Gulch and eventually flows into Chattanooga. Pass another picnic table and at 0.2 mile bear right as the

Chickamauga Gulch

trail turns off the road to ascend the boulder-strewn slope. The trail climbs to a dirt road at 0.4 mile.

The trail follows this road to the left where it narrows as you cross a small creek, dry in summer. Pass below a rock bluff and come to a crossing of Hogskin Branch at 0.7 mile. The water dances down a jumble of boulders and in dry weather flows under rocks at the crossing. The Hogskin Branch Loop then turns left off the old road while the Stevenson Branch Trail stays straight ahead. The loop descends the slope and recrosses Hogskin Branch to reach creek level at the old road on which you began the hike. There, to the right, you can walk down to the creek for a good view of the deep, narrow Chickamauga Gulch. Turn left up the old road to get back to the trailhead at 1.5 miles.

To walk the Stevenson Branch Trail, stay straight on the dirt road where the Hogskin Branch Loop turns off to the left. At 1.0 mile, pass piers that served as the foundation for a tipple, a large contraption that separated coal mined in the area. Later, curve left as you rockhop a creek with a nice waterfall up to the right. Watch for openings in the trees with views down the gorge.

At 1.1 miles, pass an opening to a coal mine that penetrates the coal layer just below the sandstone rim of the gorge. The road fades away as you continue along a path. Pass another mine opening with a coal pile at its mouth.

Along the base of the bluff, watch for falling ice and debris in the freezing and thawing of winter. There's a junction at 1.8 miles. A short trail leads down the slope to the edge of the creek. To the right, stairs, bridges, and switchbacks take you up the rock wall to connect with another old mine road. To the right, the road leads 1.5 miles to the boundary of the pocket wilderness, where the road is gated. Turn left on the old road to continue the Stevenson Branch Trail.

At 2.1 miles, pass through an old rock fall that has blocked the road and then through a coal mine area, where you'll see several mine openings in the rock bluff. Stay to the left below a coal pile. Pass over a berm at 2.4 miles. At 2.9 miles a short side path left leads down to an overlook. At 3.0 miles is a cascading stream where the trail turns left off the old road and descends the slope, passing a couple of small waterfalls, and then crosses the stream. The trail continues on to reach creek level and a ford of Stevenson Branch into a camping area, with Cooper Creek on the other side, at 3.9 miles.

Map 8. Prentice Cooper State Forest and Wildlife Management Area

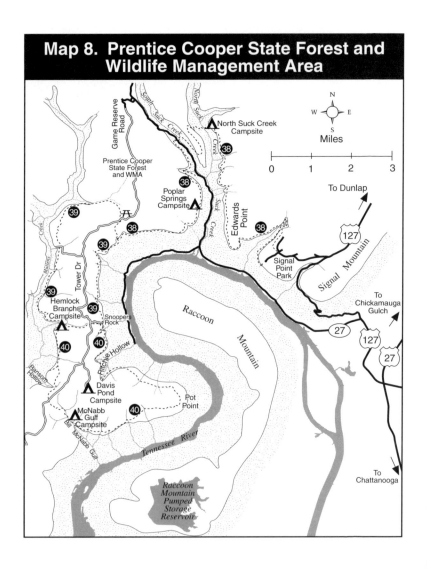

PRENTICE COOPER STATE FOREST AND WILDLIFE MANAGEMENT AREA

On the southern end of Walden Ridge, Prentice Cooper State Forest and Wildlife Management Area occupies the rim of the plateau above the Tennessee River Gorge. Here the Tennessee River cuts through the Cumberland Plateau, separating Walden Ridge from Lookout and Raccoon Mountains to the south and creating a 1,200-foot-deep gorge thought to be the fourth largest in the eastern United States. Trails along the rim of the gorge offer unequaled panoramic views from scattered overlooks.

38 | CUMBERLAND TRAIL (PRENTICE COOPER STATE FOREST SECTION)

Distance: 13.7 miles one way (Indian Rock House 0.7 mile one way; Edwards Point 2.5 miles one way from Signal Point end)
Difficulty: Moderate
Elevation Change: 500 ft
Cautions: Creek crossings, steep ascents and descents, rocky sections, briers, poison ivy, overgrown in places, ticks in summer
Connections: Mullens Cove Loop, Bee Branch Loop

Attractions: Numerous cascading streams, tall bluffs with rock formations, and spectacular views of the Tennessee River Gorge adorn this section of the Cumberland Trail through Prentice Cooper State Forest, named for a former governor. Edwards Point offers a view down the river gorge to the nearby city of Chattanooga. Most of Edwards Point was purchased in 1993 by the Tennessee River Gorge Trust, formed to protect a 26-mile stretch of this river gorge where it cuts through Walden Ridge. The trail ends at Signal Point Park on Signal Mountain. Camping is available at Poplar Springs Campsite and at North Suck Creek Campsite.

Trailhead: Drive south on US 27 to its junction with US 127 near Chattanooga and turn northwest. At 1.6 miles, turn left on TN 27. The road follows the river and at 4.0 miles turns up Suck Creek and begins an ascent of the plateau. At 5.6 miles, you'll see a small pulloff on the right and then just beyond on the left, you might catch a glimpse of blue blazes marking secondary access to the Cumberland Trail. At 6.2 miles, steps on the left show where the trail crosses the highway. At 8.1 miles, turn left on Choctaw Trail Road and then stay left. At 8.3 miles, turn left on Game Reserve Road to enter Prentice Cooper State Forest and Wildlife Management Area. The road becomes gravel; you'll find trailhead parking on the right at 11.4 miles at a small picnic area. There is hunting in the state forest. The trail system is closed west of TN 27 during deer season in the fall and turkey season in the spring.

You can get to the other end of the trail at Signal Point Park by staying on US 127 north instead of turning on TN 27. Climb the plateau to the town of Signal Mountain. At 4.7 miles from the junction of US 27 and US 127, turn left on Signal Mountain Boulevard and left on Mississippi Avenue, join James Boulevard, and then turn left at the Alexian Brothers retirement and health care complex; the older building on the corner was once the Signal Mountain Inn. At 6.1 miles, enter Signal Point Park, part of the Chickamauga and Chattanooga National Military Park. As you walk down to the overlook of the Tennessee River Gorge, you'll see the end of the Cumberland Trail to your right.

Tennessee River Gorge

Description: From the Prentice Cooper parking area, walk across the gravel road to pick up the trail. This first part of the Cumberland Trail is also part of the Mullens Cove Loop (Hike 39).

The trail descends gradually through a hardwood forest marked by white blazes. At 0.5 mile, cross a dirt road and continue until you reach a bluff, where the trail turns right and descends through a crack in the rock. The trail then curves left to a junction at 0.7 mile. To the right is the Mullens Cove Loop. Turn left. Pass an overhang that's called Indian Rock House.

The trail parallels the Tennessee River upstream. At 1.2 miles, pass straight across an open area; do not turn up left. At 1.4 miles, cross a stream with a small waterfall up to the left.

At 2.2 miles the trail curves north and follows Suck Creek away from the Tennessee River. The creek gets its name from a whirlpool that formed where the waters of the creek collided with the river. Boats got caught in The Suck until it was flooded out by the waters backed up by Hale Bar Dam and later by Nickajack Dam on the river.

The trail curves up left to cross first a small creek and then a bridge over Sulphur Branch at 2.6 miles. On the other side, turn up left for a few yards and then turn right. At 3.0 miles, walk up stone steps and pass left through a crack in the rock wall. At the top, the trail curves right along the bluff.

At 3.3 miles is a junction with the Poplar Springs Campsite 0.1 mile to the left; look for water at the spring, which is to the left just before the campsite after you cross two dirt roads. To the right at the junction, Lawsons Rock affords a view of the confluence of Suck Creek with the Tennessee River. Stay straight to continue on the Cumberland Trail. Descend, skirting an old road on the left, to stone steps at 3.6 miles that lead down to metal and wood stairs that take you farther down the bluff. The trail continues up the Suck Creek Gorge.

At 4.7 miles is a junction at a creek crossing. To the right, you can follow the blue blazes downstream half a mile to emerge on TN 27 at a secondary access point. Stay straight on the main trail and rockhop the stream. On the other side, bear right uphill. You'll eventually parallel TN 27 and then descend to cross a shallow stream and follow it downstream to turn left and descend to the stairs that step down to TN 27 at 5.6 miles.

Cross TN 27 and hike to the right down the road several yards to where the trail continues east by dropping off the road down wooden stairs to a bridge crossing of South Suck Creek. Make a steep ascent back to the top of the plateau. At 5.7 miles, the trail switchbacks right. Continue up an old roadbed and enter a passageway between bluffs created by a small creek. The trail continues up to emerge from the passage and top the ridge at an old roadbed at 6.0 miles. Turn left. Watch for the turn off the road to the right at 6.1 miles.

The trail descends gradually to cross a small stream at 6.3 miles. At 6.5 miles watch for a natural bridge over a sinkhole to the left. Then begin a more steep descent toward North Suck Creek; make several switchbacks.

View from Edwards Point

Nearer the creek, the slope is dotted with white, purple, and pink hepatica in spring. Cross a suspension bridge over North Suck Creek at 7.0 miles. On the other side lies the North Suck Creek Campsite.

Turn right after the bridge crossing. Pass through laurel and curve left to begin the steep ascent back to the plateautop. Make numerous switchbacks and finally reach the rim at 7.4 miles at Umbrella Rock, a thick pedestal topped by a large stone block. The trail turns right.

As you hike along the rim of the gorge, you'll occasionally see red blazes on trees marking the boundary of the state forest. At 10.3 miles the trail crosses bare rock and affords a view of where Suck Creek joins the Tennessee River. At 10.8 miles, the trail curves left along the Tennessee River

Gorge. The trail dips and comes up to a road; turn right. If you are hiking the trail in reverse, this turn down is easy to miss.

Right along the road, descend to Edwards Point at 11.0 miles. A spectacular view east down the river gorge ends with the city of Chattanooga in the distance.

From Edwards Point, walk back up the road and then to the right. Curve left at another overlook on a point and then another at 11.1 miles as the trail turns left up Middle Creek Gorge. The trail drops through rocks at 11.3 miles and passes upstream of a tributary that forms a waterfall into the gorge that can be seen once you are on the other side. Cross the stream above a small waterfall. Passing farther up Middle Creek Gorge, cross several small streams to an overlook at 11.6 miles. Across the gorge, you'll see the Alexian Brothers complex.

The trail drops to cross a small stream at 11.8 miles that flows out of rocks to the left. Turn right downstream to where the creek flows through Lockharts Arch, a true natural bridge spanning a water course. Up from here, the trail turns to the right down the slope to what appears to be a trail junction. To the right is simply a path to the creek on the other side of the arch. Turn left here. If you are hiking in reverse, watch for this turn up the slope. At 12.0 miles, notice up to the left an arch in formation where erosion has opened two holes through the ledge.

The trail now descends; at 12.3 miles, turn right at a junction with the blue-blazed Bee Branch Loop to the left. That trail circles Rainbow Lake, a recreation lake for the old Signal Mountain Inn, created by a dam just upstream. The loop first passes an orange-blazed side trail that leads up to Shackleford Ridge Road and will eventually connect with a new county park. The Bee Branch Loop continues upstream to ford Middle Creek on the upper end and ascend out of the gorge 2.0 miles to a trailhead on Ohio Avenue, which is the extension of James Boulevard past the Alexian Brothers complex; the trailhead is just past the complex and has a large entrance gate to the Rainbow Lake Wilderness. The trail ties in with old paths that pass a stone chimney, concrete picnic tables, and a covered spring that were part of the resort area around the Signal Mountain Inn.

On the main trail, at the junction with the Bee Branch Loop, turn right to descend to a suspension bridge over Middle Creek at 12.4 miles. This bridge and other improvements were completed by the Cumberland Trail Conference that is establishing the Cumberland Trail north to south along the Cumberland Plateau in Tennessee.

On the other side, one of the spur trails off the Bee Branch Loop has descended to rejoin the Cumberland Trail, so you could have covered a loop to this point.

Turn right toward the Tennessee River Gorge. Ascend to a swinging bridge crossing of a dry drainage at 12.5 miles. At 13.0 miles, the trail crosses a rocky drainage where you can hear a waterfall in Middle Creek below; unfortunately, there is no access to view this falls, so stay on the trail. At 13.4 miles, an overlook on the right gives a great view west down the Tennessee River Gorge where the Middle Creek Gorge joins on the right. The trail passes along the bluff and at 13.6 miles turns right to make its way up through rocks, wooden stairs, and platforms while ascending the bluff of the gorge to emerge at Signal Point Park at 13.7 miles.

39 | MULLENS COVE LOOP

Distance: 10.2-mile loop (Snoopers Rock 3.4 miles one way; Hemlock Branch Campsite 4.5 miles one way)
Difficulty: Moderate
Elevation Change: 500 ft
Cautions: Stream crossings, steep ascents and descents, rocky
Connections: Cumberland Trail, Pot Point Loop

Attractions: This loop offers views of the Tennessee River Gorge, rock bluffs, and cascading streams. The bare rock promontory of Snoopers Rock offers a wide view of the Tennessee River Gorge, and Mullens Cove Overlook affords a view of Mullens Cove where it joins the river gorge. Camping is available at Hemlock Branch Campsite.

Trailhead: Drive south on US 27 to its junction with US 127 near Chattanooga and turn northwest. At 1.6 miles, turn left on TN 27. At 8.1 miles, turn left on Choctaw Trail Road and then stay left. At 8.3 miles, turn left on Game Reserve Road to enter Prentice Cooper State Forest and Wildlife Management Area. The road becomes gravel; you'll find trailhead parking on the right at 11.4 miles at a picnic area.

Directions: From the trailhead, the Mullens Cove Loop coincides with the Cumberland Trail (Hike 38) east across the road and into the woods. The trail reaches the bluff and descends through a rock passageway to a junction at 0.7 mile. To the left, the Cumberland Trail passes Indian Rock House and continues on. Turn right at this junction to walk the Mullens Cove Loop, marked with white blazes.

The trail parallels the bluff to cross a small stream at 1.0 mile and then turns up right and with switchbacks ascends back to the top of the bluff. The trail parallels the bluff with occasional views through the trees of the Tennessee River Gorge, occasionally dipping into low areas and sometimes bearing right to cross small streams.

At 1.6 miles, descend to cross Haley Branch on stepping stones and turn left downstream to cross larger and smaller branches of the creek; at 1.8 miles, cross a washed-out road. Then watch for a turn up right after crossing the trace of a road that comes down from the right. Below the bluff, cross a couple of small creeks and at 2.0 miles turn right up through rocks to the top and along the bluff again.

Finally, at 3.4 miles Snoopers Rock affords a wide view of the Tennessee River Gorge and Raccoon Mountain across the river. Here the trail turns right up to the end of a gravel road, which is the trailhead parking for the Pot Point Loop (Hike 40). Just after you get on the road, the trail turns off left to a junction with the Pot Point Loop, which turns left on an old road; head straight across the old road to stay on the Mullens Cove Loop.

Follow a small creek to your left upstream. The trail passes through a drainage area on rocks and then curves right at a pond and ascends to cross Tower Drive, the continuation of Game Reserve Road in the state forest, at 3.7 miles. From the road, descend along a small drainage and cross small streams to eventually parallel Hemlock Branch downstream. From Snoopers Rock the Mullens Cove Loop converges with the upper end of the Pot Point Loop. At 4.3 miles is a junction where the Pot Point Loop turns left uphill to leave the Mullens Cove Loop, which turns down right to the Hemlock Branch Campsite beside the creek.

Snoopers Rock

Rockhop Hemlock Branch and continue on the Mullens Cove Loop up-hill to connect with a washed-out road; turn left. Then watch for a right turn off the road. The trail heads up a slope to cross a small stream and reach a junction with a short side path to Mullens Cove Overlook at 4.7 miles. The steep side path takes you down to a high bluff view of this tribu-tary cove of the Tennessee River Gorge.

From the overlook, the trail heads up Mullens Cove along the bluff, with occasional views. Walk up a steep section to pass below rimrock and then curve right up a stream with a small waterfall to cross above the falls at 4.9 miles. The trail makes a steep descent into the cove to get below the rock wall that forms the bluff. Follow along the base of the rock wall, working your way through boulders, sometimes against the bluff. Watch for falling ice in the freezing and thawing of winter. In wet weather, falling water sprinkles into alcoves in the rimrock. At 5.4 miles, the trail curves around a corner of rock under a tall overhang and begins a gradual ascent to the top of the bluff; some sections get steep. Along the plateau surface again, bear right to cross several small streams as you once more parallel Mullens Cove.

At 6.2 miles, the trail descends right to cross a creek and then heads upstream to cross a larger creek. Soon after, watch for a turn left uphill; a path continues straight where hikers have missed this turn, so watch for the blazes. Begin a descent at 6.8 miles across a slope and curve right to-ward a creek, then make a couple of switchbacks to drop and cross a cas-cading stream, then step up to Haley Road at 7.0 miles. Turn right up the gravel road.

At 7.1 miles, turn left off the road and switchback up to cross a small stream. Make several more switchbacks to regain the plateautop before curving right up a small stream and then swinging left to cross and return to paralleling Mullens Cove. Cross more small streams and the trace of a road at 7.9 miles and a more obvious old road at 8.0 miles as you swing in and out along the edge of the cove.

At 8.8 miles, begin a descent into the drainage of Short Creek, a tribu-tary of Mullens Creek. Bear right up the cove as the trail descends through switchbacks and across rocks and down stone steps. Once you are near the stream, turn right to continue upstream and bear right several more times up through rocks until you curve left to stay with Short Creek; keep an eye on the blazes through all this meandering. After the left turn, cross a small tributary at 9.3 miles where the creek contains a deep pool. From here along the creek, you'll see more deep pools and cascades that make a great desti-nation for picnicking and wading in the pools on a short day trip, if you hike the trail in the reverse direction.

The trail crosses a small tributary and then bears right up the slope to cross another small stream and continue up the slope steeply to a left turn at 9.4 miles. Bear right to cross an old road and then cross a small stream. The trail continues up through the woods and then drops into a ravine at 10.0 miles. Bear left and walk up to emerge at the trailhead at 10.2 miles.

40 | POT POINT LOOP

Distance: 11.9-mile loop (Natural Bridge 2.8 miles one way; Ransom Hollow Overlook 2.2 miles one way in reverse)
Difficulty: Moderate
Elevation Change: 400 ft
Cautions: Stream crossings, faint path
Connections: Mullens Cove Loop

Attractions: This loop hike offers grand views of the Tennessee River Gorge and takes you over a large natural bridge. There's a view of Raccoon Mountain across the river gorge. In the mountain, the Tennesse Valley Authority (TVA) has its Raccoon Mountain Pumped Storage Plant; the utility pumps water to a storage lake on top of the mountain when there's plenty of electricity and sends it back down through the mountain to generate electricity in times of energy demand. Ransom Hollow Overlook is one of the best views in the region. Along the trail, camping is available at McNabb Gulf Campsite and Hemlock Branch Campsite.

Trailhead: Drive south on US 27 to its junction with US 127 near Chattanooga and turn northwest. At 1.6 miles, turn left on TN 27. At 8.1 miles, turn left on Choctaw Trail Road and then stay left. At 8.3 miles, turn left on Game Reserve Road to enter Prentice Cooper State Forest and Wildlife Management Area. The road becomes gravel; you'll find trailhead parking on the right at 11.4 miles at a picnic area, where the Cumberland Trail (Hike 38) and Mullens Cove Loop (Hike 39) begin. Continue down Tower Drive, which is the continuation of Game Reserve Road through the state forest. After a lookout tower, pass through a gate that on rare occasions is closed for ice or for turkey nesting. At 3.0 miles turn left down Snoopers Rock Road an additional 0.3 mile, where you'll reach parking for Snoopers Rock and the Pot Point Loop. The Mullens Cove Loop connects with the Pot Point Loop here at Snoopers Rock. (If you have not seen the view, you should walk out to the edge of the gorge on the Mullens Cove Loop before beginning the hike.) Just into the woods on the south side of the parking area, you'll see the junction of the loop at a small side road where you can turn left or go straight ahead. Turn left down the road to hike the Pot Point Loop clockwise.

Description: Cross a branch of Muddy Creek and continue up the road. At 0.2 mile, cross Muddy Creek and turn upstream to a sharp turn left uphill. Then at 0.3 mile watch for the trail to turn left off the road on a footpath. The trail now follows the outline of the gorge rim, dipping frequently to cross drainages. The trail gets faint, especially with leaf cover in winter, so keep an eye on the path.

Ransom Hollow Overlook

At 0.7 mile, watch for a turn up right and climb steeply to a switchback left. Begin a curve right into Ritchie Hollow, which has two lobes; cross streams at the head of the lobes at 1.2 miles and 1.6 miles. As you walk back toward the river gorge, notice the formations of rimrock up to your right.

At 2.0 miles, the trail bears right up through rocks and curves right to climb to the top of the plateau, then switches left back to the gorge rim, where you'll have occasional views, especially in winter. At 2.8 miles, a path leads left to a bare rock promontory that is surrounded by trees. Immediately after, drop to walk across the top of a natural bridge. Just on the other side, you can scramble down a chute to get to the bottom, or if you don't want to slide down on your rear, you can continue on to the next drainage and turn left downstream and swing around to get back to the bridge, an impressive 30-foot-high span of sandstone.

The next section of trail meanders through the woods, crossing numerous drainages. At 3.8 miles, join the trace of an old road for a short distance. At 4.0 miles, after crossing through a drainage, watch to bear left up rocks. Swing through a couple of hollows; at 4.9 miles, the trail crosses Pot Point Road, which leads off Tower Drive (there's no view up the road to the left). Continue straight and cross the road again to walk across this headland that gets its name from a rapids, called The Pot, that was once in the Tennessee River below this point of land; the rapids is now flooded by Nickajack Lake. Cross the trace of an old road that once led out to the point.

The trail curves west to follow the gorge rim in this meander of the river. At 5.4 miles watch for a right turn. The trail passes through pine woods along the rim. Then at 6.1 miles, cross a stream near a dirt road, turn left downstream, and make your way to a side path to Raccoon Mountain Overlook at 6.4 miles. The mountain stands across the Tennessee River Gorge. You'll see an opening at the foot of the mountain where water pours out when TVA is producing electricity.

Continuing on the main trail, cross a stream and then drop through a hollow at 6.5 miles. Cross a couple of drainages and then head up a rock passageway to bear left and then right to an old road; look for the trail continuing straight. Bear right across a slide area to cross a stream on boulders below a small waterfall at 7.6 miles.

The trail then curves up Bill McNabb Gulf. Notice the large hemlocks. At 8.1 miles the trail drops to creek level with a low overhang on the right. Up the creek, cross a side stream skipping down numerous rock steps, pass several low waterfalls in the creek, and reach McNabb Gulf Campsite at 8.2 miles.

Continuing up the gulf, cross the main creek three times and then make a steep climb with switchbacks to cross Tower Drive at 8.9 miles. Reenter the woods a few feet to the right. As you descend from the road, watch for a left turn in the trail at 9.0 miles. The trail curves right when you reach the head of Ransom Hollow. Swing around the head of the hollow and cross a dirt road at 9.7 miles. But first turn left a few yards down the road and then right off the road, following the blue blazes 0.1 mile down to the Ransom Hollow Overlook, which offers a long-distance view of Mullens Cove joining the Tennessee River.

Back at the road crossing, continue on the main trail, which now heads up Mullens Cove. At 9.9 miles, the trail curves right to a cascading stream, turns up to cross the stream and pass around a huge boulder through a rock passageway, then turns right. The way is not marked clearly, but around the boulder you'll pick up the trail again. Notice the waterfall up at the rim.

Continue up Mullens Cove; cross small drainages. Descending, the trail turns left at 10.7 miles. Then watch for a right curve at 10.8 miles. Continuing to descend, reach a junction with the Mullens Cove Loop at 11.0 miles. (Hemlock Branch Campsite is just down the trail to the left.) Turn right to complete the Pot Point Loop, which along this section coincides with the lower part of the Mullens Cove Loop. Ascend, crossing some small creeks, to cross Tower Drive at 11.6 miles and close the loop at Snoopers Rock at 11.9 miles.

APPENDIX: ADDRESSES AND PHONE NUMBERS

Bowater Inc.
Forest Products Division
Calhoun Woodlands Operations
5020 Highway 11 South
Calhoun, TN 37309
423-336-7205

Cumberland Mountain State Rustic Park
24 Office Drive
Crossville, TN 38555
931-484-6138

Dutch Maid Bakery
P.O. Box 487
Tracy City, TN 37387
931-592-3171

Edgeworth Inn
P.O. Box 340
Monteagle, TN 37356
931-924-2669

Fall Creek Falls State Resort Park
Route 3, Box 300
Pikeville, TN 37367
931-881-3297
Betty Dunn Nature Center: 931-881-5708

Franklin State Forest
Tennessee Division of Forestry
169065 South Pittsburg Road
Sewanee, TN 37375
931-598-5507

North Gate Lodge
P.O. Box 858
Monteagle, TN 37356
931-924-2799

Prentice Cooper State Forest
Tennessee Division of Forestry
P.O. Box 160
Hixson, TN 37343
423-634-3091

Sewanee Outing Program
The University of the South
735 University Avenue
Sewanee, TN 37375-1000
931-598-1214

South Cumberland Recreation Area
Route 1, Box 2196
Monteagle, TN 37356
931-924-2980
Savage Gulf Ranger Station: 931-779-3532
Stone Door Ranger Station: 931-692-3887

INDEX

ABOUT THE AUTHOR

Russ Manning began his career as a science writer, but for the past ten years he has devoted his attention to travel and outdoor subjects. He has authored several books about the Southeast, including *75 Hikes in Virginia's Shenandoah National Park; 100 Trails of the Big South Fork: Tennessee and Kentucky;* and *Exploring the Big South Fork: A Handbook to the National River and Recreation Area.* He has also written over 200 articles for such magazines as *Outside, BACKPACKER, The Tennessee Conservationist, Appalachia,* and *Environmental Ethics.*

THE MOUNTAINEERS, founded in 1906, is a nonprofit outdoor activity and conservation club, whose mission is "to explore, study, preserve, and enjoy the natural beauty of the outdoors. . . . " Based in Seattle, Washington, the club is now the third-largest such organization in the United States, with 15,000 members and five branches throughout Washington State.

The Mountaineers sponsors both classes and year-round outdoor activities in the Pacific Northwest, which include hiking, mountain climbing, ski-touring, snowshoeing, bicycling, camping, kayaking and canoeing, nature study, sailing, and adventure travel. The club's conservation division supports environmental causes through educational activities, sponsoring legislation, and presenting informational programs. All club activities are led by skilled, experienced volunteers, who are dedicated to promoting safe and responsible enjoyment and preservation of the outdoors.

If you would like to participate in these organized outdoor activities or the club's programs, consider a membership in The Mountaineers. For information and an application, write or call The Mountaineers, Club Headquarters, 300 Third Avenue West, Seattle, Washington 98119; (206) 284-6310.

The Mountaineers Books, an active, nonprofit publishing program of the club, produces guidebooks, instructional texts, historical works, natural history guides, and works on environmental conservation. All books produced by The Mountaineers are aimed at fulfilling the club's mission.

Send or call for our catalog of more than 300 outdoor titles:

 The Mountaineers Books
1001 SW Klickitat Way, Suite 201
Seattle, WA 98134
1-800-553-4453

mbooks@mountaineers.org
www.mountaineersbooks.org

Other titles you may enjoy from The Mountaineers:

100 HIKES™ IN THE GREAT SMOKY MOUNTAINS NATIONAL PARK,
2d Ed., *Russ Manning*
Escape the crowds with the best backcountry trail advice for the Smoky Mountains. This completely updated and expanded guide offers more than 30 new hikes, a mix of day hikes and overnight backpack trips, and expanded natural history and background information on the area, making it the most complete guidebook to the region.

100 CLASSIC HIKES IN™ WASHINGTON: North Cascades, Olympics, Mount
Rainier & South Cascades, Alpine Lakes, Glacier Peak,
Ira Spring & Harvey Manning
A full-color guide to Washington's finest trails. The essential classic for hiking this picturesque state including maps, photos, and full details you need to plan the perfect trip.

100 HIKES IN™ SERIES: These are our fully-detailed, best-selling hiking guides with complete descriptions, maps, and photos. Chock-full of trail data, safety tips, and wilderness etiquette.
100 HIKES IN™ THE ALPS, 2d Ed.
100 HIKES IN™ COLORADO
100 HIKES IN™ OREGON
100 HIKES IN™ ARIZONA
100 HIKES IN™ NORTHERN CALIFORNIA
100 HIKES IN™ WASHINGTON'S ALPINE LAKES, 2d Ed.

EVERYDAY WISDOM: 1001 Expert Tips for Hikers, *Karen Berger*
Expert tips and tricks for hikers and backpackers selected from one of the most popular *BACKPACKER* Magazine columns. A one-stop, easy-to-use collection of practical advice, time-saving tips, problem-solving techniques and brilliant improvisations to show hikers how to make their own way, and make do, in the backcountry.

BACKCOUNTRY MEDICAL GUIDE, 2d Ed, *Peter Steele, M.D.*
A pocket-sized, comprehensive medical guide for backcountry emergencies. Explains what to include in your first-aid kit and covers all types of injuries from major to minor.

GPS MADE EASY: Using Global Positioning Systems in the Outdoors, 2d Ed.,
Lawrence Letham
Never get lost in the outdoors again! This revised edition includes extensive new material on using GPS with maps and in rough terrain.

OUTDOOR LEADERSHIP: Technique, Common Sense & Self Confidence,
John Graham
A practical guide to the skills, attitudes, and inner resources needed to be an effective leader at any level. Advice, anecdotes, and sidebars by noted leaders for all endeavors and vocations.